Sweet Wolf

On Robert McDowell's poetry

"If you're a poet looking for a writing mentor a la Natalie Goldberg, do yourself a favor and pick up McDowell's book, *Poetry as Spiritual Practice: Reading, Writing and Using Poetry in Your Daily Rituals, Aspirations and Intentions* (Free Press/Simon & Schuster)."

–Chris Watson, *Santa Cruz Sentinel*

On *Quiet Money:*

"A witty, lyrical and very un-academic poem about a bootlegger named Joe who flies the Atlantic round-trip, while Lindbergh is flying it one-way."

—*Current & Choice, Washington Post Book World*

"McDowell's poems—arresting, humorous, and strangely surrealistic—recall the work of poets like George Hitchcock, Charles Bukowski, and the early Robert Creeley—an intriguing first book, original in its phrasing and unfailingly sensitive to the pathos and humor that define our lives."

—Daniel L. Guillory, *Library Journal*

"This fresh, uncompromising voice will be greeted with cheers by readers who have been turned off by the ornate pretentiousness of so much contemporary poetry. Gifted with a novelistic grasp of exactly what it is like to be a twentieth-century American, Robert McDowell is interested in other people, not just himself."

—Frederick Morgan, Poet & Editor, *The Hudson Review*

"Robert McDowell's narrative poems are strangely compelling, adding up to an utterly original sense of the world, one brushed clean of all cant, all obscurity and confusion...Dazzling!"

—Jay Parini

"There are fine things in this debut collection."

—*New York Times Book Review*

"...extraordinary first book of poems—compelling, innovative, demanding but clear."

—Philip Miller, *New Letters Book Review*

"...the masterpiece of the book is *The Origin of Fear*...Much of the power of this stunning, compassionate poem derives from its tight and muscular blank verse. As the end of the poem nears, the lines become more emphatically end stopped, leading up to the three short sentences all contained in the last line. The result is a hair-raising conclusion. In the page margins around *The Origin of Fear* I find I've made, repeatedly, this critical appraisal: 'Wow!'"

—Andrew Hudgins, *The Hudson Review*

"McDowell has written some remarkable poems about the contemporary scene...His work is immediate, concerned with technologies of the now. Behind the characters who rehearse their lives is the massive power of political parties, economic influences...framed by his skills, his narrative force."

—John Millett, *Poetry Australia*

"...Narrative poems that entertain, amuse and enrich...a blank-verse lyrical magic does occur, as does a fine originality..."

—Robert Peters, *Los Angeles Times Book Review*

"Anyone who thought poetry was to be read, not enjoyed, should get this book...Perhaps these (poems) have a distant affinity to Frost's narratives, though they are urban middle-class American and zippier. They are poetic conceptions, not just yarns, about mysterious, unique, but representative lives."

—Herbert Lomas, *Ambit* (England)

"This is how McDowell's poetry is—vivid, rambunctious and specific. Nothing is left obscured by a mist of private or mythological references. You know what this guy is talking about. And although the situations in these poems are mundane, they often lead to scenes poignant with a sense of mystery, a sense that our old, familiar world is an unspeakably strange place in which to live."

—Mark O'Brien, *The Fessenden Review*

"McDowell's voice seems surprisingly mature. In *Quiet Money*, his technique hardly ever fails him...Perhaps the rarest quality in writers is vision, a unifying compulsion that produces insight, and McDowell appears to have plenty of it. He brings to his poems an unusually hearty experience."

—David Mason, *Sewanee Review*

"This writing goes a long way to restoring the credibility of narrative in verse. If it is to be restored it must deal with events such as this—not epic journeys across the plains, but modern scenes with language such as people use...McDowell's first collection of poems signals a change: poetry is leaving the academy."

—Louis Simpson, *Washington Post Book World*

On *The Diviners*

"McDowell unites two renascences in American poetry by writing a long narrative poem in a regular form, blank verse...The whole poem resembles a very good novel-in-stories..."

—Ray Olson, *Booklist*

On Chapter One of *The Diviners* in a review of *The Best American Poetry, 1989*:

"Other contributions...suggest that some of the best American poetry in the future will be written by poets who have simply brushed aside Derridean anxieties...to write poems with a strong narrative line... These poems may have their own, more hidden sophistication, which they use to evoke a sense of American landscape, culture and history. Robert McDowell's The Fifties, for instance, has the scope of a novel and uses effects learned from cinema and Expressionist drama as well as poetry."

—Ian Gregson, *Los Angeles Times*

"McDowell is more than the most interesting young poet to have emerged in the U.S.A. recently, he is also the prophet of shortish narrative poetry..."

—Herbert Lomas, *Ambit*

"The great value of *The Diviners* is that it will provoke discussion about the difference between poetry and prose. The language, rhythm and, most importantly, Robert McDowell's ability to evoke a character or scene in a few lines makes this work definitively poetic."

—Sarah McNicol, *School Librarian*

"The urge to tell stories has always been strong in America. It is the forgotten side to the Modernist coin, which has been lying with its abstract 'tail' up for too long; Robert McDowell reminds us that there is a human head underneath."

—John Greening, *Acumen* (England)

"Uncannily intuitive...McDowell's imagery is fresh and contemporary...Anyone interested in what's happening in American poetry today will wish to look into the new narrative poetry, and *The Diviners* is a fine place to start."

—Robert Phillips, *Houston Chronicle*

"There is an extraordinary fantasy sequence on the wife's dreams about her amputated arm when she is dying of cancer, then the son about his mother after her death: 'He thinks/of how in life she settled inside herself,/Then settled up with him before its close./He finds some hope in that'."

—*Orbis* (England)

"*The Diviners* furnishes much of the weight and complexity of a novel and does so with the impressive swiftness of a poet's thought."

—Fred Chappell, *The Georgia Review*

"That another kind of good poet should begin to emerge as the boomers mature is a reasonable expectation. That expectation is confirmed in the work of McDowell...work that is, like the Muse invoked by Milton in *Il Penseroso*, 'sober, steadfast, and demure.' Nothing in recent poetry would lead us to expect a revolution so quiet, so civil, so decent, and so precisely suited to our needs."
—Thomas M. Disch, *The Hudson Review*

On *On Foot, In Flames*:

"*On Foot, in Flames* is filled with loneliness, with the knowledge that 'the world dismantles us', but it's also prayerful, its music an affirmation that threads through even the narratives of violence and betrayal. This is a religious book in the best sense, fusing matter and spirit, ultimately, achingly human."
—Kim Addonizio

"Working in the narrative tradition of Robinson, Frost, and Jeffers, Robert McDowell is a leading figure in the expansive poetry movement. His narrative poems deliver the depth and complexity of a novel with a cinematic swiftness. They are accessible, graceful, spiritual without pretension, inhabited by characters tethered to the world."
—the Publisher, University of Pittsburgh Press

Following a trajectory from apocalypse to redemption, Story Line press founder Robert McDowell's third collection invites readers to go "into the writing where anything/ Can happen." *On Foot, in Flames* is filled with "a sweet sighing/ From the souls of trees" and "recollections of the days when you/ Surprised yourself with competence, even grace." McDowell appeals to grace in part as a response to violence, as in his depiction of working in a slaughterhouse "Stitched into gloves and apron,/ Lye-spattered, soaked with grease,/ I feed my machine 1,200 hides a day./ Sometimes I think this was the neck, this the tail" or in three blank-verse monologues that witness, among other things, violence against women.

—*Publishers Weekly*

Story Line is the indicative name of the small press McDowell launched 18 years ago to publish new narrative, formal verse. His own long poems tell stories, and his short ones are vignettes that pique the reader's narrative imagination...The longish "Sisters" is an all-too-realistic cognate of the Hollywood feminist fantasy *Thelma and Louise*; in it, murder by a woman answers long-standing personal provocation instead of abstract "women's rage." The longer "Red Foxes" tells an everyday tragedy—loss of the family farm by a couple with a school-age daughter—illuminated by flashes of subdued nature mysticism and a bleakly consoling encounter as the family drives away at the end. The longest poem, "The Pact," a slightly ghoulish story of rural adultery, shows McDowell venturing artfully on the terrain of the dour twentieth-century narrative master, Robinson Jeffers. Very impressive.

—*Ray Olson, Booklist*

"I am caught up again and again in McDowell's strong narrative line. Whether he's reshaping an old myth or detailing an actual event, this poet is a storyteller at the top of his form."

—Maxine Kumin

"The elegant decorum of McDowell's poems is intimately responsive to their subject, which is how the spirit inhabits the subtle hells and heavens of domestic life. On the surface, these poems seem easy reveries, hymns to family and farm, human yearnings toward God. But they are also an ambitious scrutiny of those subjects, tough-minded and honest."

—Chase Twichell

On *The World Next to This One*:

"Robert McDowell's powerful narrative poems are among the best written over the last fifty years. His para-poems here extend the prose poem with incisive, probing clarity and startling wit."

—Ai

"His is the very spirit of poetry. Robert McDowell is a wordsmith and a soul crafter of the highest order."

—Dr. Jean Houston

"*All I Took with the Sun* is the best poem of its kind I've read by a non-Asian poet."

—Garrett Hongo

Sweet Wolf

Selected & New Poems

Robert McDowell

Homestead Lighthouse Press
Grants Pass, Oregon

Sweet Wolf: Selected & New Poems copyright © Robert McDowell, 2021, Homestead Lighthouse Press, First Edition

All rights reserved. No part of this book may be reproduced or transmitted in any form without the prior written permission of the publisher.

Library of Congress Cataloging-in-Publication Data Pending

Names: McDowell, Robert, 1953-author.

Library of Congress Control Number 2020951812

ISBN 978-1-950475-012-4 (cloth) 978-1-950475-13-1 (paper) 978-1-950475-14-8 (ebook)

Homestead Lighthouse Press
1668 NE Foothill Boulevard
Unit A
Grants Pass, OR 97526
www.homesteadlighthousepress.com

Distributed by Homestead Lighthouse Press, Daedalus Distribution, Amazon.com, Barnes & Noble

Cover art & Book Design: Ray Rhamey, Ashland, OR
Author photo: Jim Hair.

Homestead Lighthouse Press gratefully acknowledges the generous support of its readers and patrons.

Many of these poems appeared in the following books:

Quiet Money (Henry Holt & Company, Inc.)
The Diviners (Peterloo Poets, England)
The Pact (Aralia Press)
At the House of the Tin Man (Chowder Press)
On Foot, In Flames (University of Pittsburgh Press)
The World Next to This One (Salmon Poetry, Ireland)

Anthologies:
Under 35 (Anchor Books)
The Best American Poetry
Longman Anthology of Poetry (Pearson)
Amerikanische Lyrik (Philipp Reclam jun. Stuttgart)
The Book of Irish American Poetry (University of Notre Dame Press)
The Norton Anthology (W.W. Norton)
Place of Passage: Contemporary Catholic Poetry (Story Line Press)
Story Hour (Story Line Press)
Poetry as Spiritual Practice (Free Press/Simon & Schuster)
New Poets of the American West (Many Voices Press)

Magazines:
Boulevard, Connecticut Review, Crosscurrents, Janus, Kayak, Little Magazine, Madoc, MARGIE, NER/BLQ, New Jersey Poetry Journal, Poetry, Poetry Australia, Poetry New York, Poetry Northwest, Prairie Schooner, Pulpsmith, Solo, Sycamore Review, The Chowder Review, The Formalist, The Hudson Review, The Kenyon Review, The Ohio Review, The New Criterion, The Sewanee Review, The Wolfian, Vivace, Washington Review, West Coast Poetry Review

The author is grateful to the editors and publishers for their support.

Contents

Someplace Between Story and Song: Introduction by Chad Abushsnab — xi

from *Quiet Money* — 1
Quiet Money — 2
Working a #30 Sash Tool, Thinking About the Pope — 17
The Cop from Traffic Accident Control — 20
Into a Cordless Phone — 22
After the Money's Gone — 26
The Malady Lingers On — 28
The Liberated Bowler — 32
How Does It Look to You? — 34
The Backward Strut — 38
The Librarian After Hours — 40
Ballad of Maritime Mike — 43
Poppies — 47
The Origin of Fear — 49

from *The Diviners* — 57
The Nineties — 58

from *On Foot, In Flames* — 71
Courting Emily — 72
Where and What You Are — 75
The Valley of the In-Betweens — 76
The Red Ball — 77
The Pact — 78
There Is — 93

Levels of Intersection	*94*
Elegy in August for Beverly	*95*
Grateful	*96*
My Bird, Your Face	*97*
For Liam (1949-2007)	*98*
For Lysa, That She May Rise Early	*101*
After	*102*
Travelers	*103*
The Discovery	*104*
This Time of Year	*105*
At Home with Doll-Face	*106*
Paranoid	*107*
Women and Men	*108*
The Sheep That Feeds You	*110*
October	*112*
Daughter	*113*
Red Foxes	*115*
Prayer for the Harvest	*127*
Prayers That Open Heaven	*128*
from *The World Next to This One*	*129*
From the Green Pen	*130*
All I Took with the Sun	*132*
A Woman and Man Stand Alone in the Street	*144*
So That's It	*146*
Bum God	*147*
Hold Your Breath	*149*
Lying Close Is a Crawling in	*151*
Talking with the Dead	*153*
Reminder	*155*

Meeting Jesus	*156*
Autistic Boy	*158*
Horse Sense	*160*
You	*161*
Chess	*162*
Nicely Done	*164*
Baby on Fire	*168*
Let's Say	*170*
Raccoon and Possum	*171*
Circle	*172*
Sand Tray	*174*
When the Talking Goes Away Pantoum	*176*
Paddleboat	*177*
The Day after Labor Day	*178*
Dog and Poet	*181*
A Wee Tonic	*182*
Young Richard on the Road	*183*
New Poems	185
Acorn, the Clown	*186*
Career Change	*194*
Bukowski—When I Met Him	*196*
Pissed at Bukowski	*198*
Boxing with Sylvia Beach	*199*
A Great Adventure	*200*
Diving in Super Cave for Divine Feminine	*203*
The Great Translator	*204*
Mise en Abyme	*205*
Gang of Chimps	*206*
The Man Who Took Over	*209*

War	*211*
Dancing Truth	*212*
Meteni For AL	*214*
If Only for FP	*216*
Late Maker of Chariots	*218*
The Bishnoi Trees	*219*
Father's Mourning Wood	*221*
Like Our Fathers before Us	*223*
Rock Gongs	*224*
Paterson, the Movie	*226*
Shit	*230*
Cat Killers	*231*
Growing	*234*
Her Uncles Come at Christmas	*236*
Her Shoe, Her Foot	*238*
When The Reaper: Ode to a Lit Mag	*240*
The Calapooia Flood	*242*
Joe	*248*
Poetry & Literacy	*249*
Anacampserote	*250*
The ANS	*252*
The Woman in the Painting	*254*
No Little Genius	*258*
Virginia Downstream	*260*
Virginia's Way	*262*
The body is a mighty feint	*263*
About the author	*264*

Is there not a sweet wolf within us that demands its food?
—Emily Dickinson

*for family, friends, ghosts, animals, trees, flowers,
ponds, rivers, lakes & magic that sweeten the years*

Robert McDowell

The Poetry Portal: Healing & Adventuring Within

"Heavenly Hurt, it gives us –
We can find no scar,
But internal difference –
Where the Meanings, are –"

Emily Dickinson's observation became Robert McDowell's directive, his odyssey launch to explore *internal difference,* to discover and illuminate that mysterious place *Where the Meanings, are*—. Poetry is witnessing. It is song, the song in the story; it is dance, Beauty and the Truth. It is the realm where, as Virginia Woolf put it, *"Now then is my chance to find out what is of great importance and I must be careful and tell no lies".* Poetry, as Robert Frost said, is *'taking the road less traveled by',* the life-changing decision that *'makes all the difference'.* The poem, conceived in fever dreams in and between this world and the next, written and written again and again in vulnerable isolation, finds its readers, if readers there are, in an act of making community with diverse others, with the heron and the owl, the poppy and the rose, the tiger and the fox, the bee, the lamb, the bear and the wolf. *"Blame it or praise it, there is no denying the wild horse in us,"* said Woolf, and she is right. Poetry is the wild horse running free in each of us. *"This is the life itself."*

Someplace Between Story and Song:
An Introduction to Sweet Wolf: Selected & New Poems

Chad Abushanab, Assistant Professor of English, Bemidji State University

When I was at the Sewanee Writer's Conference in 2015, B.H. Fairchild gave a craft lecture in which he discussed—among other things—the lyrical and narrative natures of poetry. Particularly, Fairchild stressed that these two kinds of unfolding must always co-exist in poems, albeit in varying ratios. There are no purely "lyric" poems, just as there are no purely "narrative" poems; rather, a poem seeks to find a space between lyric and narrative and use elements of these qualities to push towards meaning. The finest poets spend their careers exploring this spectrum.

By and large, contemporary poetry has landed squarely in the territory of lyricism. This is not to say that contemporary poetry eschews moments of narrative cohesion. But it is obvious the short lyric (and, for longer pieces, associative movement based on an opening up of the lyric moment) is experiencing a period of overwhelming popularity. Narrative inevitably exists in these poems, but there is a strong sense that sound is taking precedent as the guiding principle of composition. Rare, then, is the contemporary poet who gives privilege to narrative as the engine inside the poem. Rarer still is the poet who masters both the art of deep, complex narrative and moments of mystical musicality wherein truths feel just beneath the illusion of sense. It's for this reason the greatest joy in seeing the best of Robert McDowell's poetic career distilled between the pages of *Sweet Wolf* is witnessing the massive swaths of ground McDowell covered between the poles of lyric and narrative. Throughout *Sweet Wolf*, we see his prowess on the level of the individual poem as well as within the selections from each collection represented.

The very best narrative poems often contain the depths of long form fiction realized through a tightly controlled economy of language, and McDowell's 1987 debut *Quiet Money* is a master class in this regard (and a bonafide literary miracle given the rocky providence of its initial publication). The eponymous poem—a long narrative piece almost in the Frostian tradition about a bootlegger and transatlantic pilot in the days before Lindberg—river-runs many of the techniques found in McDowell's poetry throughout the following three decades, among them a powerful tension between humor and solemnity. The poem, whose themes of distances both physical and emotional are rendered with subtle clarity, moves between passages of masterful character building to moments of quiet musicality.

Narrative-minded verse is often criticized as putting too much emphasis on story at the expense of musicality. Nothing could be further from the truth in McDowell's early poems. Rather, we see sure-footed dedication to the music of language. Among his strengths is his ability to reflect drama through line breaks and enjambment, such as these lines from "Quiet Money," where we see the pilot at the moment of deciding to head out across the sea:

> He lingers, checking the Wright Whirlwind engine.
> The headwinds say *look out*;
> His patience says, *take off*.
> Far to the north the lights of Jersey sparkle,
> Calming down.

The rhythmic diminishment here stands in for the moment of rest before the pilot bounds to the cockpit and rises skyward, the rhythm then bounces along to the cadence of childhood play:

> He scrambles up the wing, his perch,
> One step from home. The cockpit
> Makes him think of the backyards of boyhood.
> Clearing the stand of trees at the field's far edge,
> Joe banks to the left, circling the field,
> And levels out heading northeast.
> He likes that initial turn, getting the feel of it,
> Feeling the earthbound tug slip away.

The gentle interplay of information and musicality is a defining feature of "Quiet Money," as well as many of the other poems from this early collection. "The Cop from Traffic Accident Control" delivers brutal, visceral detail in a manner at once both coolly detached and delightfully ornate. "The Origin of Fear" revels in the difficult language of philosophy while dancing, irregular rhythms lead us over the edge of lines again and again.

The selection from *The Diviners*, from the section called "The Nineties," demonstrates McDowell's mastery of meter, gliding effortlessly through blank verse, which is delightfully aware of its own arrangement:

> Tom and Elaine went out to fetch some money;
> Elaine and Tom came back with bucket loads.
> Tom thinks how like a nursery rhyme it is.
> "What do we want?" Tom asks. Elaine only shrugs.
> She reaches for his hand and they lie down.

McDowell's second collection resembles Frost's great poetic dramas in more ways than one. Indeed, beyond both poets' masterful wielding of the blank verse line for dynamic effect, both have a unique understanding of the mechanisms of human relationships under duress, how we manage to love our way through despair. This selection from "The Nineties" concludes with the death of Tom's father. In a particularly Frostian moment, Tom remembers his father's eccentricity fondly:

"Well, he didn't suffer,"

Tom says. "So like him to hurry even death."

But as with Frost's hired man, we are pulled between memory and the moment at hand, the reality of his death, and the physicality in which it presents itself, albeit with McDowell's signature tension between laughter and tears:

Tom grins a little, recalling his father's face.

"It looked good on him. Don't you agree?"

With all that make-up on he dropped some years.

Here, the poet taps into something painfully human: to hurt is a grace as there is untold tenderness to behold at the edges of pain. Moments such as these resonate throughout McDowell's career, following him into the 21st century and a decided leap into even more lyrical waters.

Having proven himself a master of the blank verse narrative, the early 2000's saw McDowell begin his swing into the direction of more pointed lyricism with *On Foot, In Flames*. The very title indicates an interest in the strength of the image, the associations made through affective response in addition to semantic meaning. In this collection, poems more fully rooted in the lyric tradition sit side by side with narrative excursions that call to mind the most well-crafted moments of McDowell's early career. The selection here pays homage to both modes, giving equal weight to each, in what feels like a statement on the importance of these two forces in tension.

Poems such as "Women and Men," "Prayer for the Harvest," and "Prayers that Open Heaven" have the quality of incantation. These verses lean heavily into their musicality and seek truth through discovery. "Prayers that Open Heaven" embodies this spirit, as the poem itself presents the speaker cycling through phrases in search of "the words and guides you should follow." In this poem and others, McDowell follows his intuition beyond narrative (though without ever losing interest in an element of "story," as even with "Prayers that Open Heaven" there are enough concrete details to discern a narrative consciousness in the speaker).

Of course, there are also poems that call more clearly to mind McDowell's narrative penchant. The longer piece "Red Foxes" harkens back to the poems of *Quiet Money*. But more fascinating still are the poems that occupy a middle ground of lyric and narrative—those that more fully explore the expanse between story and music. Perhaps my favorite poem from this selection of *On Foot, In Flames* is "Daughter." The blend of musical repetition and narrative richness is nothing short of exquisite. Each stanza begins with a variation on the declaration "This is the day," while adding a new narrative element to the poem, pushing the speaker's address to his daughter even further, in a sense discovering what the speaker means to say, developing "the close-up murmur/ Of your parent's prayers."

The World Next to This One further develops this tension between lyric moments and narrative propulsion, further integrating the two modes into individual poems, ultimately presenting their interplay beyond the level of the book. Having already experimented with this kind of tension in *On Foot, In Flames*, McDowell brings a new focus on formal invention to his palette, as well. The earlier comparison to Frost is a fair one, I think. But moving through McDowell's later collections brings to mind an even stronger precursor: the late Donald Justice. Like Justice, McDowell is something of a formal maverick in his later years, re-inviting approaches to the shape of poetry to suit each utterance. The poem that most clearly brings this all together is the episodic "All I Took with the Sun." The poem, which follows a speaker's voyage from Japan to his subsequent life in the United States in the years before and during the Second World War, is, on its face, a work rooted in narrative tradition. And yet there are moments where the language takes the driver's seat, particularly in the section titled "Hiroko's Passage." Here, the poem's blank verse breaks into dimeter lines wherein the echo of rhyme appears to determine the direction of the sentences with as much agency as the story behind the language. It is a prime example of McDowell getting lost in the music to marvelous effect:

> I knew that I
> Had traveled far
> From orphanage
> To dock, to star,
> From empty space
> And setting sun
> To this new one.

Though rooted in the narrative, this particular verse takes off on its own and revels in music and discovery—the turn "From orphanage/ To dock, to star,/ From empty space..." actually transporting us into mystery, allowing us to embody the journey.

Also represented in this selection from *The World Next to This One* are several of McDowell's prose poems: "Nicely Done," "Paddleboat," and "The Day after Labor Day." The prose poem is a curious and dynamic form, which often concentrates its energy in syntactical surprises and anaphora. It is a favorite medium for surrealism, its boundlessness and breathless nature allowing for images to run wild. McDowell's prose poems, then, are remarkable in their turn away from the fantastic in favor of the quiet drama of the domestic. In "Nicely Done," something as simple as watching a movie recommended by a friend becomes a conduit for introspection. In this piece, the prose poem form moves the speaker in and out of the world of the film, casting the action around the television as something just—if not more—cinematic than what's happening on the screen. True to the syntactic style expected from prose poems, McDowell's sentences wind around like smoke and deliver long parenthetical asides that feel very much like the mind in the act of creating. There is a feeling of improvisation in this poem that is anchored by the very deliberate crafting of sentences and the feeling of inevitability once McDowell starts to give us the big picture. Again, these grand gestures strike a delicate balance between story and song, priming us for the concluding section, *New Poems*.

This latest collection of poems sees McDowell again return to the long form voice studies of his earliest collections while introducing the careful, quiet of lyricism that has emerged over the course of his career. One cannot help but see the symmetry between *Quiet Money* and *New Poems*. But it is not a perfect symmetry. It is far more complex than that. Instead, it is like looking into a mirror that sends light over long stretches of time so that one sees a reflection slightly strange, a reflection matured. The section's opener "Acorn, the Clown," for example, bears more than a passing resemblance to the eponymous "Quiet Money" in terms of shape and interest, and yet I see meaningful growth in a style that emerged self-actualized and only became more confident throughout the years. There is, of course, the shift to the first person, cementing "Acorn" in the tradition of dramatic monologues. The advantage of this mode is opportunity for more deliberate modulation of sound, which injects the poem's narrative with a high intensity dose of lyricism:

> So, yeah, I'm saying that clowns are separated at birth
> From the truth.
>
> Jane, are you awake?

The turn, the sudden break in attention, the sound of a thought unwinding, epiphany in the making, creates lyrical peaks that are made even louder by the quiet question that follows. In searching for an analog, one can't help but think of the work of Elizabeth Bishop—another great craftsperson of the illusion of thoughts caught in the process of becoming known.

This skill is taken to even greater heights with the collection of unique (and yet connected) speakers in "The Calipooia Flood," not to mention "Waiting for the Dead" and the "Virginia" poems. These latter pieces tip fully into the lyric mode, offering up some of the most musical moments of the book—an impressive feat in a collection replete with music:

> In the deepest part the lady's voice
> *Unvanquished and unyielding*   said
> (if not to me, to whom)
> What took you so long
> This way   Come

It is quite fantastic that a poet with such a strong sense of narrative can slip so easily into these moments of pure music, where sense is almost (but not quite) beyond grasp, lost in the sound. And I believe, ultimately, this is what sets Robert McDowell apart from many of the narrative poets that precede him, and, indeed, his contemporaries. There is *mystery* that emerges from in between the certainties. In the poetry of Robert McDowell, no story is without its song, the thing that compels us forward beyond the sense of the thing into the feeling of it, that resonance of which the poet speaks in "Poetry & Literacy:"

> What sound can they make
> But an untranslatable
> Buzzing in God's ear?

from Quiet Money

"The Life so short, the craft so long to learn." — Chaucer

Quiet Money

The bootlegger opens his eyes and stares
Down the gray runway, another Wednesday.
Bony, shivering in early bathroom weather,
He gropes for a glass of rye on the windowsill
And flicks on the light. Flight day.
The weather report on the wireless is good,
Though what he sees in his shaving mirror
Makes him think of mechanical foul-ups—
A slice of wing shooting past him,
Propeller chips smacking against his goggles.

Flicking his thumb across a straight razor,
Joe tells himself it's good to feel the edge,
To remember it's only a membrane or a veil
That separates blood from the body intact.
He thinks of blood, the body breaking apart.
He imagines a membrane holding it all in.
He thinks of landing an office job and laughs,
Thinks of coffee in a field cup and he's warm.
Two alley cats howl, toppling a trash can.
"That's motivating music," he says,
And mutters the closing bars of *Over There*—.

Betty sulks in a luncheonette on Fourth.
Daubing her nose with a hankie, stirring eggs,

She wants him. She wants him everywhere.
On the bus to work she thought of telling him,
"Give it up or stop coming around,"
But the words were too heavy to carry,
Like too much weight in her handbag
Throwing off her natural stride.

Now she laughs
At the thing she'd tried last night,
Pouring so many martinis, hoping he'd nosedive
Into a bottomless sleep and miss this day.
But Joe can hold his liquor, especially when
He's talking poetry and war. Later,
Betty can't remember the hour she passed out,
Or the minute he pinned the note to her pillow.

> *See you Monday, Doll Face,*
> *With something pretty from Paris.*

* * * * *

The airstrip flags point east at a quarter to five.
Joe rubs the compass in his flight jacket pocket,
His fingers brushing the pages of Wilfred Owen,
And he's thinking of wings.
Not those of machine, but of birds,
What he'd wanted as a child

Who had loved the bird's life of recklessness
And dramatic death down a chimney
Or in the talons of a larger bird.
Walking around the plane he whistles.

"Nobody knows," he mutters, "but some Frenchmen miles away.
'Nobody crosses The Pond alone,' the experts say.
Well, I won't be rubbing their noses in it,
Though there's plenty gearing up to do just that.
Circus flyboy stuff. There's money in it,
But fame comes with it, too—a suit you can't take off."

He lingers, checking the Wright Whirlwind engine.
The headwind says *look out*;
His patience says *take off*."
Far to the north the lights of Jersey sparkle,
Calming down.

He scrambles up on the wing, his perch,
One step from home. The cockpit
Makes him think of the backyards of boyhood.
Clearing the stand of trees at the field's far edge,
Joe banks to the left, circling the field,
And levels out heading northeast.
He likes that initial turn, getting the feel of it,
Feeling the earthbound tug slip away.

He imagines gunning for stars,
But the stars are at peace, in collusion.
The sun balloons above the waterline,

The moon drops down to the sea.
Joe thinks of the money he's flying,
Of crates of cognac stacked in a French hanger.
He thinks of a present for Betty, of the life
He's making, up here, among prosperous currents.

*   *   *   *   *

She doesn't want to think of him all day,
But superstition bites. She takes off,
Daydreaming herself into flight beside him.
"Joe," she murmurs, "all I want is a home
With you on the sofa, drinking a soda."
After five, plodding home, her head
Keeps lifting to a drone that isn't there.
"Monday's not far off," she whispers.

*   *   *   *   *

Joe's gruff Parisian contact waves
As he lifts off, climbing in the wind
That will take him back to the luncheonette.
He climbs on the current and the current inside him,
The energy Betty loves him for and fears.

Twelve hours out, twenty from home,
He fights it,
The drone of the motor stirring sleep.
He regrets staying up so late the night before
Singing war songs, talking baseball

And British poets, and women—always women.
Joe nods over the controls,
But something besides sleep isn't right.
Something in the sky is wrong.

He snaps to attention, focusing
On a silver image before him, skimming the sea.
Bird, then *dolphin* occurs to him. Then *plane*.
That can't be, so he tells himself *reflection*
And conjures the creature from an old story
That snatches plane and pilot
If they fly too close to the sea.
"That can't be anyone but me," he says.
The image below him fades, heading the other way.
Joe's relieved, but that's wrong. He cups his hand
Outside to catch a breeze, to deflect it into his face,
But sleep blows through him, too.

Now he's groping for the brainstorm gadget he'd installed
Beneath his seat. He finds it, brushes against the live wire
With his wrist, and sits up, back to himself.
He's alone—as it should be.
Below him nothing angles but the sea.
Hitting fog, he pulls back on the throttle
(Like flying inside a glass of milk)
until he finds clear air at 4,500 feet.
He thinks of Betty asleep,
And of Brown and Alcock
Teaming up to cross the Atlantic first in 1919.
He thinks of them losing their bearings in fog,

Flying upside down within 500 feet of the sea.
How many times did Brown crawl out on the wing,
Wiping snow and sleet from the fuel gauge? Joe smiles.
"Those fellas made good, alright, but what for?
10,000 pounds, knighthood,
And Alcock dead in a crack-up six months later."

Good night, Irene, good night...

Joe tips his wing to Alcock
And levels out over the coast of Newfoundland.

* * * * *

Sweeping cups from the counter into a tray,
Madge winks as Joe saunters past the register.
Betty, raising a fork, freezes,
Riding out a tremor, and a wedge
Of lemon meringue free-falls to her lap.
"You can't wear your food with this," he says.
One hand rests on her shoulder,
The other sets a hatbox on the table.
Tapping the left side of his jacket
He lowers his voice. "Tonight," he says,
"I'll show you what I've got in here."
Betty's face is like clearing weather
As she preens herself in the mirror,
Admires the way she looks in a smart Parisian bonnet.
"Maybe that hat will help you see things differently,"
Joe says. Betty sits down while Joe fidgets with a cup.

"You don't look well," she says. "What's up?"

   "I pushed it to the limit on this run.
I let myself stay up all hours,
And then I couldn't hold it off—
The Sandbag Eye—I saw things.
I saw the creature from that story you hate;
I saw myself as a child, grounded in a strange neighborhood.
I saw another plane, Betty. A reflection, I guess,
But that's what shook me most. Listen,
I got a bonus for the quick turnaround.
It's more than we've ever seen.
Why don't we get hitched?
Just don't ask me to give it all up."
"I know," she says,
And hammers one hard kiss across his chapped lips.

On the street, Joe feels the slap of a newsboy's cry:

   Lindbergh Lands in Paris!

Joe whistles like a punctured tire.
Betty, nodding, hugs his arm.
"I didn't want to bring it up," she says.
Joe leans against a lamppost, staring east.

   "Lindbergh.
I never thought he'd beat them,
Byrd and the others with their bankrolls.
I knew he was in the hunt, in a quiet way,

But I never figured this.
He'll get tickertape parades and medals now,
Money and keys to the mayor's w.c.
Think of it, honey, all that brotherly love."

On the landing, at the door to her walk-up,
Betty fumbles in her purse for keys.
"At least Lindbergh's never landed *here*," Joe says.
Inside, he pulls a bottle from his duffel bag.

   "Sometimes a proud man
Doesn't wave himself around," Joe says.
"Headlines cut the pants off privacy.
They make you public, a pioneer.
I wonder if he knows what he's in for?"

Joe talks and talks
As the moon pins a spotlight on his face.
Betty wrings her hands and rocks,
The bottle open on the bureau-top,
But neither takes a drink.

              *   *   *   *   *

Past three, Joe is flying blind, questioning.
Betty's breathing is a motor in good repair.
Joe hums under his partner's sleep.
"What?" she murmurs, banking out of a dream.
"I'm thinking of getting a house in Jersey," he says,
But he's thinking of Lindbergh, too.

He's thinking of a plane below him,
Skimming the rooftops of Paris, beating him out.
"Anywhere," Betty says. "Anything you want."

What *does* he want?

Nearing five, Joe looks down at his body in a restless sleep.
Sprawling so, he looks a little like Italy on a globe.
Out of the body, a body looks that way,
A smear of papier-maché, a flare-up,
An ugly reminder on a fist of blue.
Joe, or Joe's double, wonders
If the quiet atmosphere he flew in was a cheat.
Betty, asleep, looks like a separate country.
How can she make him believe in home?
In peace? Can anyone? Undertakers, maybe—
White-jacketed illusionists keeping a low profile.
Why does Joe's double escape so many nights?
Why, when he returns, does he keep
What he's found to himself,
A country inside a country, unmapped?
The questions hound Joe out of sleep,
So wrapping himself in a blanket,
He gropes his way into a chair
And flicks on the reading lamp.
Slowly the room settles, focuses,
And he picks up a copy of *Lear*
To whisper the fool's lines, his favorites.
Their sound, the way it makes him feel,
Is enough. He rides it into the afternoon.

* * * * *

On moving day, they look like a couple
In a paperweight, their arms around each other.
Joe is Errol Flynn in a flight jacket;
Betty's lucky hair falls down like rain.

After the movers back over the curb
And putter north, the newlyweds
Climb the fire escape for a farewell drink.
"What are you thinking?" she asks.

"Nothing. Just noticing the wind,
How it's turning nasty, how I wouldn't wait."
The winner in the paperweight dissolves;
A hard and lonely figure takes his place.

"Joe, how long before you face it,
Before you get it straight—what it means to you?"
"What are you talking about?"
"Not what," she says. "Who."

Joe faces her. "Don't push," he says,
And suddenly he sees himself as memory,
His image fraying like tapestry.
"I hope you can take it," he says. "Your man's obscurity."

* * * * *

"Something Willy said just ticked Joe off,"

Betty tells her neighbor in the backyard.
The iron fence between them soaks up heat.
"I don't know what."

"I do," her neighbor says. "Willy was carrying on
About the Yankees and the Babe.
You know how men get hot when talking sports.
Well, Joe claimed that there were players in obscure leagues
Who were just as good as Ruth but never got the breaks.
Willy wasn't buying, and soon they were toe-to-toe.
Their faces got red, the veins in Joe's neck popped out.
I noticed that just before he did it—
Threw his glass (I swear it nicked Willy's ear) in the pool."

"That's when I came out," Betty says.
"I saw Willy's eyes get big like balloons
And Joe just turning, walking away.
He passed right by me and didn't speak,
Though I could feel anger breathing out of him.
It goes back further than the Yanks and the Babe."

A drone out of the west breaks in
And both women look up
As Betty's single-engine fly-boy tips his wing.
Anna gurgles in her playpen.
Chug, their terrier, snoozes on a plank of sunlight.
The plane levels off, descending
To the airstrip a couple of miles away.
Betty holds her breath. *Irrational,*
She tells herself, but she can't help it.

Only when he turns their Silver Ghost
Up the drive will the moment be enough,
His coming back in one piece
To lift Anna off his knee,
Catching her as she parachutes back.

*   *   *   *   *

"I had a case of the yips for years," Joe says.
His nephew, Charley, sips lemonade and nods,
Not knowing what Joe means. He lets him talk.

"After we got hitched,
The weather always indicated stay.
So, I'd scrub a couple of flights a month,
Then two a week, and pretty soon
I was on the ground more hours
Than I was logging in my plane.
Imagine what that did to me!
You never feel the same
Once you've cut through weather
And known it topside. You miss
The motion, the nerve-and-bone collision.

"How many nights did I rock in my chair,
Spending in my head the cash I'd make
As soon as I got home safe? And *safe*—
That word would take me like a haunting
As I'd fall back in this room knowing where I was.
I had it, yes. The Yank dream,

No rain, no sleet, no public pilot
Cutting his silver trail under me,
No flight I couldn't roundtrip in a day.
When I couldn't sleep I'd rock.
I don't know how I put her through
Those shifting moods, but Betty was great.
She'd touch me—stop me, really—
'Level out,' she'd murmur,
But if she strayed too long I'd veer off course again,
My throttle hand squeezing nothing,
Making fingernail imprints on its palm.

"I had to face it,
The need for something to run up against,
A glass door, a garage wall, a chirping neighbor,
An impassive, staring hero on the front page.
Anna helped, and the dog, and this place,
But I needed more. I got it, too.
It's sad to think of it now."

At sixteen, Charley perks up to the promise
Of a sad story. He refills his glass,
And without asking does the same for Joe.

"You're a little young to recall firsthand
the scene I'm thinking of.
It was March of '32.
The Lindberghs had a house not far from here
Outside of Hopewell—ironic name!
The papers served up their grief like daily bread.

We memorized photos of ladders
And footprints in the mud,
A ransom note on the windowsill.
The baby, as near as we could tell,
Was stuffed, still sleeping, in a burlap bag.
'It looks like the work of pros,' the cops said,
Which was good for the kid's sake.

"And then the waiting. Ten weeks of dying,
Ten weeks of cranks and comforters,
Wheels (the cops called the crazies *wheels*) and volunteers.
I flew some for the cops, you know,
Shooting down false leads. It made me sick
Each time I landed with nothing to offer Lindbergh
But a negative shake of my head.
I'll never get the look on his face out of my head.
It was a mid-Atlantic look, your plane out of fuel.
The clocks ground on but didn't move.
Mail flowed into their house like lava,
And all for nothing. Cruelty.
The body turned up in the woods
A few miles away—and this is the awful part—
He'd been dead since that first night.
The ladder-man dropped the burlap sack,
And the baby's head struck a window ledge.
Imagine how the 'nappers must have felt!

"And Lindbergh. How far out,
in after-years, did he push himself to feel secure?
And the rest of us...how many couldn't sleep

For fear of waking without sons or daughters?
We learned to love the sounds of words
That covered us—words like *lock* and *alarm*,
And we raised you on them.
Now you can't look strangers in the eye,
And there may be secrets
You can't even share with your closest friend.

"Son, you have to lose to win.
That notion settled in us
And we passed it on to you.
Thank God. You know what it meant to me?
My daughter safe, first of all,
And all of it, really.
I spent so many nights in her room
Just watching her sleep,
Convincing myself no gang would take her
From me—ex-fly-boy, average businessman—
And suddenly I was happy.
My life's course felt fair.
I thought of fame and money, and still do,
How what we do to get them can make us sorry."

Working a #30 Sash Tool, Thinking About the Pope

"There is no hurt in my profession," Buck muttered,
Checking a door for skippers.
He felt ravenous for spaghetti
And glanced at his watch—10:30.
"I'm tough," he mumbled, "I can take it."
He worked like that awhile, taunted
By the vision of a savory meat sauce.

Meanwhile the radio updated the Pope's condition.
His Holiness was dead, was gravely wounded.
The Pope escaped serious injury.
Bystanders were injured or praying.
One bullet was fired and there were many,
The shooter acted alone and with others.

Buck was furious. He hated
The voices feeding him news, and he
Hated the wimps whining for gun control.
He spat out the word *foreigners* and grumbled,
Thinking how they talked funny and caused trouble.

Working, hurting, Buck came up with a program of blood control.
He wondered exactly how his country might do that
And did not think of his Scotch and German ancestors.
He was American, the best damn painter in Los Angeles.

Didn't he mix his own colors?
Hadn't he won the unofficial contest?

"Nobody will shoot me in this line," Buck stammered,
Then he crossed himself and prayed for the Pope.
Twenty feet up on the ladder he felt close to God and thought
Of the Pope falling into the arms of his secretary.
Had he fallen like a lovesick girl,
Or like a child walking a ledge,
Astonished at missing a step?

These soft images were strange, even foreign.
Flustered, Buck shook himself thinking,
"He fell like any man shot in a jeep."
But an inside voice kept saying

> *The Pope is not a man.*

Buck finished off a run of putty
And spoke as wood might speak—

> "He fell."

To calm himself, Buck thought about his wife,
Happy in her kitchen, who had probably
Turned the radio off, hating the terror
And intrusion on her easy listening.
He imagined her greeting him in the driveway,
A woman priding herself on never making
Unpleasant connections. He'd puff up like bread
In her arms and she'd say something like

> "Isn't it awful?

Guess what we're having for dinner?"

At sixteen, hurling a javelin into the sun,
I never imagined the look I'm wearing now.

Some nights I dream I hide myself in the park,
Coming among the lovers like cold rain.
Arriving late, pulling them from the wreckage,
Sometimes I dream I hear their loved ones weeping.
And what they say of me is true:
That I arrive, a spit-and-polish mop-up,
Reinstated, man with a cancelled expression
And a flat-top haircut, out of date.

Into a Cordless Phone
for MJ

On Reelection Night the news was bad.
He called his oldest friend. They talked for hours,
Cursing groundhogs chewing up the line,
Transcontinental gobblers. His friend was trying
Out a cordless phone.
                      "I'm moving now,"
He said, pushing through the backscreen door.

"I cut my grass early this afternoon.
It looks just like the flattop cut you wore
In school. Suzy loved to skate her palm
Across your varsity plateau until
You graduated to the shaggy look.
I'm not the one who got invited to
Her parents' cabin at Lake Arrowhead!
Her family OK'd only right-wing nerds
Like Eddie Planck and Nehemiah Boone.
So tell me who you voted for. You won't?
Go walk along an unemployment line
And see how they take the news. You've done it? Where!"

He didn't catch the response of the unemployed
Because the cordless voice had broken up.

I have no one, he thought, and glanced at stars
As if an operator might appear.
Instead a shooting star arced east to west
And something to his inner ear said *Walk*.
So, heading west he crossed his neighbor's yard.
He stopped to stroke a basset hound, then dialed
His cordless phone and said hello. A sound
Washed over static, buried it in verbs—
"Run! Pack! Get your things and go!"
The dog he was scratching yelped and shook its head.
The crash of something falling shot from the house.
"Hello!" he said to the phone. "Hello! Hello!"
A wave of static rolled in to answer him.

He hurried past the house and crossed the street
To Earhart Park. By the lake the phone was silent.
Only laughter from a grove off to his right
Came in to him. He heard a bottle break
And hurried on until he faced her statue.
Staring up at the missing aviatrix
He raised his phone and spoke. "Come in," he said,
"For God's sake tell me where you are tonight."
The statue stared as if he didn't exist,
And nothing on his phone disputed it.
Farther down the path he chose a spot
To lean against a pole and warm his face
In yellow light that made the stars go out.

He thought of spy planes grazing the bleak Pacific;
He thought of rumors never verified
And wandered into the Children's Area
Where he sat on a swing and dialed his boyhood home.
Was it his mother he was speaking to?
He talked and talked about a day in school,
Then caught himself, fearing local news:

MAN ON SWING CALLS HOME ON CORDLESS PHONE

His cordless phone was dead, his mother, too.
Amelia hadn't answered. No one spoke.

He left the park and crossed Elm Avenue,
Then circled round the Billings' swimming pool.
Maybe water cleared its frequency,
Because his phone was rafting one low voice:
"You can't sit out there every night," it said.
"Nothing you can do will bring him back."
Another voice was sobbing while it spoke,
As soft as water lapping in the pool.
Then crying leveled off in a woman's voice.
"I just ran in to get the phone," she said.
"He was sitting in his playpen in the sun."
Her voice collapsed as he pushed through a gate.

The smell of garbage billowed out of cans.
His phone was mad with voices changing every
Twenty steps or so: *Sausage and anchovies—*
Feed the dog or shoot it! I don't care!—

Sweet Wolf

I told you never play with Daddy's eyes!—
Take this, please, and try to get some sleep.—

He thought he should hang up but couldn't bring
Himself to disconnect his neighborhood.
He ducked a squad car, squatting behind a hedge,
And tried to eavesdrop on their radio.
He dialed 911 and said *Police*;
Another voice screamed *Fire* and he ran.
Crossing a familiar lawn he hopped a fence,
Then crept up to a door and dialed his phone.
"Hello," he whispered, "can you hear me now?"
His daughter's southern drawl was sweet with sleep.
"Go call your mother to the phone," he said.
His wife came on. She said his voice was odd,
"Like someone's sitting in a well," she said.
His friend's long-distance, earnest voice broke in
But faded after shouting the word *Where*.
He said to his wife "I will not sleep tonight,"
But he dropped the phone on the lawn and went inside.

After the Money's Gone

Hector could not help himself
When he thought of kites, meadows, changeable winds.
Like his namesake he could not win.
When he landed a job, it was always the same.
He would stick it out for a week or two
Then begin to miss his morning bus.
His boss would spot him in the park,
Red in the face, chugging over hills.
Hector would wind in his skein of string
Like a terminal patient, the pink slip
Stuffed in his shirt pocket, and head for home.

His wife was worth half a dozen jobs.
That's how many he lost before she left him.
"Plant yourself," his buddy told him over beer.
"Hug your swatch of earth
Like it's your own skin.
That's what a woman wants in her man."
Hector knew if he went home he'd stay up
Watching reruns of shows he didn't care for.
He thought of going to church,
But the air in church was bad. He knew
If he thought of his wife he'd begin to cry.

His buddy tossed money on the bar, said goodnight.
"What is it women want?" Hector muttered.
He rubbed the stubble on his face
And thought of bad weather robbing the sky of kites.
"I feel dry though I drink and drink," he said.
He thought of words that could change the look on his face.
He thought of balsa wood and paper,
He thought of wind, miles of white string.
To say their names over and over almost made him smile.
He did not touch another drop that night,
And he was on his way to the park before sunrise.

The Malady Lingers On
for TR

Bill Davis. The name a clairvoyant
Spelled in the palm of her hand.
Tina makes like it's no big deal,
But she's willing, even desperate,
To meet the man the seer describes.
That is enough to bring her to Madame Faye.
That and a carload of friends needing breaks
From husbands who never call them *princess* anymore.

Tina's story began on a farm
In southern Illinois in the 1950s.
She fears that it stops there, too.
At age 5, turning cartwheels on her bed,
She crashed through a window.
The damage to herself was minor
And her mother wept. Daddy paddled her behind.
Come Sunday the family knelt in church.

She was guilty. She knew it.
She was guilty undressing dolls in her sister's bedroom,
Guilty as a cheerleader at 16.
That was tough competition for prayer—
Human pyramids and athletes sassy in their sweats.

But she was not long satisfied with kids her age.
She was after something else
And found it with a local boy just out of the Marines.
Sleek as a halfback, the boy was all God and Country.
When he said, in so many words, that he *was* a god
She said *why not* and let him in.
In no time at all the mother of many children
And living in the suburbs (and not yet 22) she said,
"it felt like the beginning of a story."

    Bill Davis, home from work, uncaps a beer
And reads *The Wall Street Journal*. The economy
Is bad and he feels it in his gut.
He replays the day's events, his public self.
"Nobody knows my true worth," he muses,
"Least of all myself." He says,
"The only thing worse than breaking down
In public is breaking down when you're alone."
The thought clasps him until well after sunset.

"You don't know what a help you are," he says to Cat.
"Evenings when I cannot tell the house
From all the others on the block
I look for you in the window.
Are you looking for me? I wish you'd speak."

Night after night he watches the news with Cat,
Which is to say alone, or reads a book,
Or works his thumbs and ponders what he was—
A kid who one day thought he'd spruce the fish pond up
By pouring antiseptics in it.
Nobody said a word but he was proud
Until the fish surfaced, belly-up and bloated.

Tina says to her friends, "Let's grab a drink."
Inside the bar she heads for the Ladies' Room
Where she looks up Davis in the phone book.
"Hundreds," she hisses, "and a dozen Williams."
She clasps her handbag shut as if slamming a door
And stalks out to a margarita.

Meanwhile, Bill is bored with books and TV.
If a stranger called and said his name came up
In her hand that afternoon would he believe it?
He suffers from indigestion and rubs his face,
Thinking he needs a shave. He thinks of Cat,
But he will not shave for her.
He wonders if he should sit on her lap.
"Maybe I should just tie her up," he mutters,
and wonders if *he* would like to be tied up.
He thinks of his escape trumpeted on the news.
His chest swells.

Tina bites her lower lip
And stamps out her cigarette.
"Butt-end of another boring day," she says,
Then weaves out through the parking lot.

After several struggling minutes Bill is ready—
Hog-tied he kneels on a kitchen chair,
A noose around his neck,
The rope knotted round a water pipe.
Sockless, red in the face, he tries
To free his hands. The chair rocks.

Maybe a neighbor glancing through a window
Will spot him and call the cops.
Or Tina may arrive, checking addresses
From the page she ripped out of the phone book.
Bill and Tina will turn up eventually,
But in what condition?
Neither one is thrilled about tonight.

The Liberated Bowler

Never at the Olympics will she wed,
And never in grandmother's dress
(Who could not break 200 for her life).
Never in church will Ethel forfeit her name,
The pews a refuge for losers and bad sports.
She will take her man in Lane 3
Or not at all, the preacher
In a black coat behind a scorer's table.

"At last, a wife who's functional," Bill says.
"Goodbye to rented shoes and stippled balls;
Goodbye to the miserable misdirection of my life."
He cannot wait for the ceremony to end,
For the honeymoon—two weeks of bowling—to commence.
"Starting out in training is good for a marriage," he says.
In his mind he masters impossible splits,
The stare, stride and pure release of a champ.

Meanwhile Ethel's mother weeps.
"America," Ethel murmurs lovingly to Bill.
Her eyes are moist, and she rubs the ring
Made out of bits of her lucky turquois ball.
When both have said *I do* they bowl a game for luck
While fellow bowlers sing and toss rice.
"I am happy," Ethel says. "Almost like bowling a perfect game."
The preacher, signing the license, records a strike.

Six months later Bill has trouble sleeping.
Her words as they left the alley haunt him.
"In a year I'll count on you for back-up.
A solid 185 will do."
He had asked what she would do
If his game dipped below 185,
And shuddered when she did not laugh.
"Your average can only go up," she'd said.

On their first anniversary Ethel cannot sleep.
She sits at the kitchen table making little mounds
Out of cigarette ash. Bill, a heavy drinker,
Lies on the bed like defeat.
"I kept my patience for the longest time," she mutters,
"But when bowling for the championship he rolled
A gutter-ball in the tenth I lost it."
Her voice is split in two. She cannot pick it up.

Today Bill dabbles in real estate
And Ethel spends most evenings tuning her game.
The marriage that shook Rockport is memory.
"I want a wife who's functional at something *I* do well,"
Bill tells his buddies during Happy Hour.
Ethel shaves the headpin, picking up a split,
And wishes for a man who can take it,
This thing she does so well.

How Does It Look to You?

    Listen, friend, I saw him use a Bic
To light his pipe. We'd just climbed into the car,
I looked over and poof! He'd lost his face.
That damn thing going off in a closed car
Took me back to popguns we'd packed in school,
But there he was, thirty, burning up!
We'd warned him, too, to chuck that flamethrower,
But he'd crank it up as high as it would go
And laugh at smokers jerking back their heads.
I grabbed it from him once and turned it down,
But in his hands again he wound it up.
Why? *Protection*, he would say sometimes,
Sometimes *It's a conversation starter.*
Every now and then he'd say real low
How he hated folks with bedroom lashes.
He had them, too! But now he needn't worry.

    I hit-and-ran red lights to Emergency
Then drove for his wife who screamed when we rushed in.
After the scream, she ran. In high heels yet!
It took me a city block to reach for her,
And when I did she took a swing at me
With her purse, raising a grape on the tip of my ear.
The purse went down, and every item in it
Scattered across concrete. I had her wrists,
Then two men dropped a dolly and had me.

My arms were tied like pretzels up my back,
And something hard and heavy pressed my neck.
One guy hissed *I got him. Get police!*
I saw some shoes run off. I tried to speak.
But all I could make was a little croaking sound.
From where I lay I couldn't see high heels
But I could hear her screaming *Watch His Face!*
My mind was fuzzy by the time I heard
A squad car stop. The handcuffs bit but good,
Strong hands rolled me over, sat me up,
And sun-glare off a badge blinded me.
A voice said *After the lady's purse, creep?*
I caught my wind, laughing long and loud.
My shoulder caught a jab from a nightstick
And that shrill voice was screaming *Not His Face!*

When I could talk again I didn't laugh,
Remembering how I'd seen a joke blow up.
I stared at knees, explained the accident,
The way the victim's wife had run away
And what she'd done to me. They stood me up.
One cop behind me took away his charms
And six of us marched back to Emergency.
My friend was gone, transferred to a Burn Center,
And I thought about how much he'd laugh at me.
A doctor seconded my story.
                              I was free.

The Workboot Boys went back to their Loading Zone;
The cops took off after making apologies.
The woman got a hypo, pawed at her nose,
And even after I thought she'd gone to sleep
Made disturbing gestures toward her face—
Like someone drowsing, waving off mosquitoes.
She muttered, too. The only words I caught
Were *No* and *Face*. Not strung together, mind,
But free-floating, striking her like bites or stings.

    Outside, the sun was hot. The gutter stunk.
My earlobe tingled—antiseptic wash—
My shoulder ached. I hunted up a drink
And thought of my pal and his wife.
He'd recover, work for an agency,
And do ok with low visibility.
She might learn to look at him and smile;
She might just leave a note and walk away.
I wondered what she'd dream about that night,
But I had my face to feel and think about.
I sat there drinking until the bar closed down,
Then walked on home and put my face to bed.

I counted matches striking one by one
And finally dozed around three. I wish I hadn't.
I felt her high heels stab my back and legs,
And she was chanting words I couldn't reach.
Then a pastor rolled me over, waving his hand
Above my face, and I was lifted up.
He placed her hand in mine, recited verse,

And married us right there in a Loading Zone!
We stood together, learning with every stroke
Our lips, chins, noses, cheeks, foreheads, hair.
A scar-faced crowd pressed all around us, moaning.
We shut our eyes.

                        She whispered *Honeymoon*
And we were checked in to a House of Mirrors.
In every room, we entered we were new.
One morning we were three feet tall and fat;
At lunch, we looked like giants with long bones;
At dinner, we admired our shoulder wings.
She said *Next week we'll open the Animal Rooms.*
Who knows how long we lived there? Long enough
To learn to love variety in looks.
Distortion is the gift of second sight.
Did I say that? Did she?

    Today I visited my trickster friend.
I got close to the bandages and talked.
He lay there like a matchbook on a street
But faintly squeezed my hand as I got up.
I knew just what that meant and called his wife.
We talked an hour. I asked her out to lunch.
Imagine where I'll take her after that.

The Backward Strut

When his telephone rings at 3 a.m.
And nobody hangs up and nobody speaks,
It comes to him that childhood
Is so remote it belongs to someone else.
Later, dozing in his favorite chair,
He dreams he can leap into moonlight
And be only vaguely aware
Of children, rebuked, taunting parents,
Of the alley crunching and gobbling, claiming its own.

Awake he sits at table and stares at the phone,
Hoping she'll unlock her language box.
He wonders what the dog knows, lying in a heap,
And the cat whose drug is an open window.
Maybe they'd like to listen to the radio,
But there's too much heartache on the air.
He feels like a man who opens a closet
To find another's clothes hanging inside.

Is he destined to live out his life
A lowercase letter among capitals?
Is he the test chemical that never pans out?
He remembers how at his christening he wiggled,
Evading the holy spray of water.

He thinks how there is no song to fit this life,
How the lyric is just like a wishbone—
A rush from the heart, a crack, and that's that.

The Librarian After Hours

She has it by heart, the mechanics of his trap,
A blood moon promising luck.
Settling onto the porch with a glass of Glen Ellen '81
She has what she needs to travel—
Good weather inside her,
True-life tales committed to memory,
Her summer guests gone home to their autumn faces.

Now she is hunting beside the pioneer
Who lived so long on opossum
He ate everything raw.
"One appetite spawns another," she says,
Nodding her head at the turn of each page
Until she wanders back, mulling over
Certain meals at which despair sat down
And seemed to crop the centerpiece.
Conversation rubbed too much skin away.
"Nobody leaves the table satisfied," she says.
Her book rides the current in her lap

And the architect comes back, picking at crepes.
"That hospital was earthquake-proof," he said,
But there were seventy people dead.
His wife, the ceramist, squeezed bread as he spoke
And shut him out with strident talk of pots

That held whatever they were meant to.
"Stop fussing with your food," she said,
Speaking too loud to spare him.

"Do you wonder what you're eating?" the hostess asked.
Not unlike the meal she served the beekeeper
Who checked a hive under the eaves and later proposed.
She made him speak of himself.
Unbuttoned by brandy and cigars
He rambled on about his lonely life among bees.
Noting how he glanced repeatedly at the phone
She sent him staggering to his car
While she rejoined her opossum-devouring pioneer.

Suddenly the midnight opossum appears,
Plodding through ivy to empty her coop of eggs.
The librarian's tidy appearance sags
As she closes her book and leans over it.
"There is no hunger like your look," she whispers.
When the trapdoor clacks she rises;
In the coop she corners her fattest red.
As she squats beside it, awash in porchlight,
The ivy-trellised cage rocks and ceases.
The red is a chaos of feathers;
Soon the opossum will twitch in a roasting pan.
If tomorrow the beekeeper calls at work,
If high school students cut up in the stacks,

She will stamp them with gentle reminders,
Then maybe invite them home for a meal.
She sees them clearly as she cooks all night—
The beekeeper retreats into reference books,
The students open their journals and disappear.

Then she punches the ticket out of herself
And pulls back the flap of a covered wagon.
She scans the nothing the future will call her land
For a glimpse of a trapper shouldering dinner.
She waits with a pot and wooden spoon
For mouths to feed, appetites to satisfy,
And says
          "I serve as an outpost, a sponge to hunger,
A scrapbook of obscure survival tips.
I am the chair with an ear,
The cook and comforter on desolation's porch.
Relax to the scratching of knives and forks,
Sweating pitchers of lemon water.
Believe that your confessions are worthy of books,
That no matter the names of courses
You are eating a marvelous story."

Ballad of Maritime Mike
For MJ

The continent depressed him,
  His scurrilous crew rolled dice.
He tuned in an old-time radio show
  And scratched the sheet for lice.

His wife was not there with him
  Though they'd married just recently.
She said if she sailed she'd become someone else—
  She said "No one means *that* to me."

He never wanted to change her,
  To make a ship's mate of his wife.
He thought of someone equal in rank,
  Bread to his butter knife.

He thought of someone equal in rank,
  A thought that made him grieve
Realizing that his wife was the kind
  Who'd pack up her lipstick and leave.

She worked in some government racket
  That doled out cheese to the poor;
She spoke of herself as a guardian of mice.
  If he giggled at that she got sore

And needled his sallow complexion,
   His risky investments gone sour.
She told him to beach his seagoing dream
   And focus on corporate power.

He put his hand in an ashtray,
   Sketched a sail on its floor,
Then hurled it through a picture window
   As she bolted the bathroom door.

She brayed abuse from the tub,
   He whined that he needed to sail
As he had in the war after submarines.
   His grip on the doorknob was frail.

His grip on himself was worse,
   Slick as a soapy plate.
When he came home late a note from his wife
   Said "I'm out on a dinner date."

In lipstick, he scrawled that he loved her
   On the medicine cabinet mirror,
Then he shuffled out with his duffle bag
   While mumbling a sailor's prayer.

He put down money on a hulk
   As big as a PT boat,
Appeared out of place in unsavory bars
   Signing crewmen who'd keep it afloat.

The best was committed to ritzy lines,
   The worst drank up his liquor.
Through shoals of ale, through a spray of darts,
   He got just what he paid for.

So, all aboard they waited
   For Providence to package a sign
In the shape of a wind from Alcoa or Sears,
   Like heartbreak the harbor was sighing.

The radio show was scratchy.
   The crew cursed, rolling dice.
The captain's ugly life reared up
   And jerked at his collar twice.

Then a spiritless fish pursued him
   With a mouth like his jilted boss.
Its teeth were grainy with dollar signs,
   Its breath an anthem of loss.

He wanted to hook that fish
   By reciting appropriate Scripture,
But the door to his learning was webby and cramped.
   He'd never been much of a reader.

Foul weather spotted his compass,
   Failure sat down on his charts.
The crew below plotted to slit his throat.
   Disaster flexed in their hearts.

Meanwhile the captain's wife
  Had hired a crack P.I.
To track him down and cuff him home.
  She'd already had a good cry.

That hunter found him, too,
  In his cabin of turtle light.
He told him that he'd been sent for;
  The captain stood up to fight.

In a minute or two they were puffing
  Like fish reeled out of the sea.
When the captain's shoulder popped he groaned
  "Look what you've done to me!"

The drive from the harbor was poignant
  As the captain blubbered and swooned.
The P.I. wiped a yawn from his face.
  He felt good. It wasn't his wound.

The captain's wife was waiting,
  Her skin looked like Singapore.
He rolled down his window and managed *hello*.
  She smiled and he wanted more.

She tucked him in bed with hot brandy,
  And said she was running late.
She said they had much to talk about
  After her dinner date.

Poppies
For Patricia McDowell Aakhus (1952-2012)

I can't find a book to help me out of where I am.
I remember the day we drove out to the fields,
Or rather the day I drove out with our friends.
You had to work, but you were with us just the same.
It was still an age of pet names and horizons.
I had been reading *The Mysterious Stranger* by Mark Twain
And I climbed each hill hoping to meet him.
Nothing could have been stranger—
The California desert a-dazzle with poppies.

Drinking beer, we thought of the Land of Oz,
Of lions, tin and straw.
Though we felt a little ashamed for thinking of them
(We were not in school any longer),
Though we were fond of reminding ourselves of what was real,
We didn't fight it when on a nearby hill we saw
A girl like you dancing in her ruby slippers.
Late in the day we split up and I climbed
Until voices called me back. Running

I was Alice pursuing the white rabbit.
When I put my foot in a hole and tumbled down
I was Jack with an empty pail of water.
Waiting for the pain to let up I imagined

Around the World in 80 Days,
My ankle soaring as crowds cheered.
Oh yes there were moments of delight,
Stories I felt a sure part of,
Days in which you and I were perfect.

The Origin of Fear

The Death Month, August, wears a driver out,
But he is almost home, speeding over
A residential street with his windows down.
A woman on a corner screams or laughs,
Her disembodied cackle crashing in.
He turns. He sees a blur of toothy face

And breaks into the sweat of an eight-year-old.
Melting down his hands run off the wheel.
He squirms against an ice chest in the back.
He fixes on the back of his mother's head
And sticking to the seat he thinks it's beautiful.
An hour goes, an hour of gas and heat
And he is moaning now, pleading for his
Angel of the Douglas Fir to take him home.
But no Angel appears. "Mother," he wants to say,
But she is driving to the radio.
There is barely room in the car for parent and child,
Barely room for the ice chest and winter coats
They'll need up north, barely room for breath.
One window, broken, swallows spanking heat.
"Hang on," his mother says. "Hang on
Until we climb out of L.A." To the child
The drive seems longer than a long, long day.
He tries to think of heroes who hang on,

But soon he retches out the broken window.
Empty then he falls back in his seat
And offers up his spirit to the sun.
He thinks he knows Extermination now.

About the time the nausea returns
The Edsel starts up 99, crossing the Grapevine.
There is nothing to see but Death hills, Death sun,
Then, miracle of miracles, Death
In images he cannot stand to look at.
Fascinated, he stares at a giant billboard
Where a woman like his mother, dressed
In black, weeps above an open casket.
A gray man in a grey suit lies inside.
Their two small grieving children flank the box
While a black oak highway trails off behind.
And over a hill, in the upper left-hand corner,
A black-cowled risen Death's Head smiles.

Now the boy can feel his own death near,
Though a merciful distraction might dismiss it.
Instead, a second billboard offers up
A scene so dark the boy stares hard to see it.
A sickly moon. A stormy hill of tombstones;
A mother-woman stands before a grave.
The boy looks at her back and feels her tears.
The chill he feels keeps growing as they come
Up on a third billboard, a fourth, a fifth,
All images of Grieving After Death.
In one a suited shadow-man walks off

With Death, his children's faces wailing as
The veiled mother-woman holds them back;
In another a white cross dwarfs the highway;
In the last the smiling Death's Head waits for traffic
Like a parent willing children home.

The boy will never sleep the same again,
Feeling kinship with the broken billboard
Boy and girl, agonizing over
How his mother and the billboard lady looked
So much alike, how the father left
The billboard family, too.
                                            But that was years ago.
Today, at thirty-two, he's driving home
While the billboard painter pours himself a drink
Down south in a hillside home, warming up
His voice for the evening air of the Coliseum.

*

The team from *People* magazine, paid
To feel this way, nod and act enthralled.
"Tell us how His word first came to you,"
The writer says. "Tell us how the artist
Turned to God."
                     Their subject preens and swallows,
Crunching up an ice cube while he thinks.
"You ever drive up north on 99?
Ever see my work before the Commission
Tore it down?"

           The *People* people stare,
All natives of the East. Their subject shrugs.

"You know I studied art in Hollywood,
Even shared a studio with Pollock.
I was in a gallery on Melrose then
And sold a painting every three or four months.
Much good it did! Jackson hit New York
And made it big but I...I was stuck.
It got so I was lucky just to eat
And then I saw the ad in the L.A. *Times*:

CALL FOR ARTISTS: OPEN COMPETITION!

"The State Highway Commission had a plan
To gag the outcry over traffic deaths
By putting up a string of nightmare billboards
Along the most fatal stretch of road in the system.
I heard a thousand artists sent in slides.
A month went by, another week. I sagged
And for the first time in my life I prayed.
Then I was called.
                    I had a week to sketch
A winning series based on traffic death.
The day of the interview my competition
Laid out gory scenes of mangled steel,
Bodies missing arms, legs, eyes—even heads!
Their colors were red, autopsy blue-and-white.
Now me, I kept my colors somber—
Blacks and grays—and focused on survivors,

The grieving Left Behind, women and children
Victimized by witnessing. I focused
On their agony and fear and on
Their grinning master, Death. I'd slow cars down
Through paralyzing shock alone! I said
'Suggestion is more awful than the crash'.

"My argument paid off. They hired me.
I had six months, a massive studio,
A vision I believed was worth my skill.
Day and night, I sketched and painted Death—
And not Death you might reason out in time.
I sketched and painted Death and then I prayed.
Michelangelo knew what I'm talking about.
My girlfriend didn't. She said she wouldn't come
To the studio anymore—*couldn't* come—
Because she woke up sweating, dreaming of Death.
One day as I was working on a child
It came to me I hadn't heard from her
In more than a week. And that, my friends, was that.
You wonder did it bother me? Not much.
When the Commission toured my studio
I felt as John the Baptist must have felt
To see the waders changing as they came.
I knew then what my life was all about.
My signs went up.
                      I laid my brushes by.
Often, I would drive up north and park
Just close enough to see the Series whole.
Exulting, I observed the drivers flinch,

Their cars slow, swerve, then pick up speed.
Face to face they'd seen what God could do!
Fatalities declined because The End
Was there on giant boards for all to see.

"I had seen. I read the Scriptures and
At night, I took an elocution class.
I perceived that I must master words.
I'd done the visual, which only reached
The few who drove that way. I dropped my friends
And spoke in bars and unemployment lines.
I pestered the press, pressuring for space
And one fine Letter to the Editor
Led to my first call to address a church.

"The pastor introduced me as a painter
Who had given up a lie for Him.
As he pointed to the ceiling I looked up,
Then took the pulpit to correct his gaffe.
Paint was the avenue He took to me;
My failed life was all I had denied.

"That little talk was good. When it was done
The congregation greeted me with a found look.
From there the invitations multiplied,
As did my following, and then my friends
From local business clubs made clear to me
The need for one sane voice to make a church.
I guess you know the TV part of it.

Today so many hide out in their homes!
I have to get to them in God's New Way."

*

Nearing ten, the tired man up north
Pours three fingers neat and pulls a downstairs
Chair before the color console screen.
Sitting in the dark, his left-hand strokes
The neutral body of remote control
And thinking of that disembodied scream
He sips his drink and presses. The screen glows,
Then hums and focuses like prophecy.
Feeling a little better, he punches through
The major network news, a canceled show
From nervous boyhood, a horror film.
He doesn't feel enough to stay with these
And turns to cable just in time to see
The L.A. Coliseum from the air.

The next shot is a close-up of a man
Whose manner seems to open like a psalm.
The viewer straightens, leaning in to it.
He tries to create distance with a curse,
But turning to other channels he comes back
To that accusing, urgent voice of doom.
The viewer paws at his stomach, feeling sick
And wonders why he just can't go to bed.
He curses the sleep, for him, that lies ahead

And thinks of words he said above a casket,
His hollow mother, rigid, facing him.
He rubs his eyes then drops his hands and stares.
Unbeliever! I know I'll pay for it.
He witnesses, he moans, he fears his bed.

from The Diviners

"It is the word of life!" the parent cried;
"This is the life itself," the boy replied.

—George Crabbe, *Peter Grimes*

The Nineties

       Elaine's next book, a thriller, outdoes the first.
The money she receives—embarrassing,
Obscene, though not without some pleasantness.
Tom thinks of that whenever he recalls
The cryptic photograph and sign at work,
Which Al put up above the employees' sink.
The photo showed a woman, pencil thin,
Her old skin sagging, a deflated leather bag.
And in gold letters the photo's caption read:

    THIS WOMAN IS AMERICAN,
    BUT SHE LOST ALL HER MONEY.
    TOO BAD! WATCH YOURSELF.
    WORK HARD AND GET SOME MONEY!

Elaine and Tom went out to fetch some money;
Elaine and Tom came back with bucket loads.
Tom thinks how like a nursery rhyme it is.
"What do we want?" Tom asks. Elaine only shrugs.
She reaches for his hand and they lie down.

In time they lounge on pillows on the floor
And watch the wall-size monitor for fun.
On channel one, the dog in section D
Rolls over, watching *Animals Today;*

In section Q a child recuperates—
He's drinking liquids, sketching body parts;
In section Z a dented housewife drinks.

"It has to be immoral, watching this."
Tom tries another channel as he speaks.
The monitor goes gray and buzzes out.

*

    Al curses The Slump sponging his assets dry
And looks out on his smaller neighborhood.
He thinks of the Lodge, looks forward to a drink.
Some take delight in whittling on him now,
But others see the dying in his face.
To them he's Boss, a harmless inside joke
Who's grateful to be asked to cock his fez
And march behind some local majorettes.
Through El Molino, the City of Industry,
He marches to the brass, on top again;
A man who makes things happen, in a baggy suit,
Appearing to strangers as he never was—
A caring man, so tender toward the poor,
The sick and needy, the workers out of luck.
Al gives a quick salute, but his eyes are dull.
He thinks of Tom, his bitch of a daughter-in-law.
They never call or line up on the street
To watch his squad of money-makers march.

This sets the subtle sneer on his tightening face.

"Another day, another disaster," he sighs.

*

Well how do you do young Willy MacBride,
Do you mind if I sit here down by your graveside—

Tom wakes up with these lyrics in the room
And tries to shake the nightmares from his head.
He wishes he could wake up once at ease,
Like long ago. The boy in Tom retreats.

Downstairs he empties powder in a glass.
He rubs his chest, imagining angina,
And quickly washes down two beta-blockers.
His mother's portrait stares, though not at him,
Its dark eyes peering into zones so deep
He cannot find some comfort there. He thinks
Of how in life she settled inside herself,
Then settled up with him before its close.
He finds some hope in that. Across the room
He leans by the door to breathe the morning in.
The sun is slowly cutting coastal fog
As late-departing, stubborn autumn birds
Wake up and sluggishly begin to caw.
Then wavy rose-light bundles over rooftops.

Terrific, for a moment, is the calm.

"Today we need an outing," says Elaine,
Who has come down from their bed. "You don't look well.
We'll take the whole day off, the two of us;
Let's tour the new exhibits of the decades."

"A day off at the History Arena?"

"Why not? We'll walk back to our childhoods."

"That's swell," Tom says. "Can we rewrite them, too?"

"Get dressed," she says.
                              Tom follows her advice.

   After the video that thoroughly
Explains the pricing and packaging of goods,
After the train museum, the phone displays
And demo cars and trucks on pedestals,
Elaine and Tom decide to walk through seasons
In the Climate Hall. They scuff at maple leaves.

"When I was a boy," Tom says, "the grown-ups said
The seasons would be constant, never changing."

"My part of town just didn't have the time
For talk like that," she says. "We took what came

Our way. You holed up in your room with books;
If that's deprived, I'd take a piece of it."

Around a corner a robot hands out coats
In snow puffed out of ventilation shafts.
They climb into a sleigh on hidden tracks.
Outside a moonlit house they pause a while,
Content among the carolers. The horse
Starts up, and soon they thaw out in a park.
They shed their coats. Tom shags a whiffle ball
A motor boy sent up with a plastic bat.
The foliage is breaking, tender renewal,
And men in Hawaiian shirts show off their lawns
While barbecues smoke up the neighborhood.
Some robot kids on bikes patrol the streets
As Tom and Elaine slow down outside a house.
Two children play on swings while mother cooks,
And all are smiling as if they've never thought
About a thing. Tom walks the gravel drive
Toward a familiar scene, a huge garage,
Its rafters cluttered, and wash that billows on
The line out back. Elaine knows when to move,
And tugging on his arm she leads him back.

Not far from home Tom lightly strokes her thigh.
She leans into his chest and he veers the car
Into a dusty eucalyptus grove.
Outside, the air is thick, medicinal.
Undressing even as they leave the car,
They kiss and lie down in a cloud of health,

But neither can claim that healing enters them.

*

    The 605 is clogged, as are the roads
In Al's uncertain head. He gazes south
And sees the cemetery sign uphill,
Its letters white, gigantic through the smog.
"My Eleanor is dead," he mutters. His hands
Make nursing movements on the steering wheel.
A siren sounds behind him, coming fast
Along the open shoulder of the road.
A muscle in Al's neck begins to ache
As he looks back, so he curses as the cops
And ambulance go hunting for a crash.
Al rubs his sagging chest to ease a cramp
And conjures up his high school coach's face.

"I hated you," Al says, "but I obeyed.
I bought the program. You taught me how to win.
But if you were so smart, how come I'm losing?"

Al doesn't feel much better with windows up.
The tinted band across the window top
Distorts the light, making mountains blue,
The unreal blue of backdrops in a movie.
Al wants the scene to shift, the plot to improve,
But he is in a still-life on this drive.
He tilts the rearview mirror to check his face;
His high cheekbones are gone, his eyebrows gray,

His lips go slack and turn a purple hue.

*

       All day Elaine and Tom drive aimlessly.
They get home late, neglect their messages
And try to sleep, but neither has success.

"I just feel lost," Elaine says. Jerking back
The sheet, she slips off her robe and slippers.
Tom sits up, says
              "Why don't you take a pill?"
Downstairs he finds her in the eating room.
"So, talk to me."

            "I'm sick of this," she says.
"We've lost what's human in the work we do,
When we despair we take forgetting pills."

"I know," Tom says. "I face it every time
I walk the halls and see the workers file
Through metal doors to fill those frigid rooms
Of icy chairs and desks like frozen meat.
I sit at one myself and think one day
Some Boss will risk it all and draft the memo
Proposing that the system be revised
For work at home, for twenty-hour weeks."

"Don't kid yourself," she says. "We're years from that.

I'm all for getting out of here. Will you?"

"But what about the movie and your books?"

"The movie will be bad. My books—who knows?"

"I suppose," Tom smiles, "we'll leave the monitor."

"Let's trash it," Elaine replies. "Let's leave it all."

The thought of shedding what they own is good,
But then Emergency is on the phone.
Tom listens, nods his head, and says ok.
He hangs the phone up quietly and waits.

"It's Al," she says. He nods in her embrace;
she thinks of wrapping one last loose end up.

*

  Al does not feel his own dismantling now,
The nauseous rush of his last cigarette.
His thinking fixes momentarily
On an interior, a lab at night.
A faceless surgeon cuts an animal,
Approaching sickness as one more job of work,
While over the door a sign in neon pink:

  It is humane (and easier) to die.

Al's mind is spinning, stopping suddenly
To make out fists above a bleeding man.
The face above the fists, Al's face, is ghoulish
In a loser's light. Its mouth is slurring speech:

> *Oh, when I drink all night I am so happy,*
> *So happy I could work the heavy bag.*

The drinking shows in his hair. The image blurs,
Yet other scenes are swift to take its place.
The chainsaw neighbor leans across a fence
To slice Al's yapping dog from snout to tail.
Then women from his hotel afternoons
Appear to probe Al's groin with knives and guns.

"What's left," they laugh, "for any girl to love?"

Then dental drills attack his weakening gums
As a voice declares
                    "You're pushing sixty-two!
You must take better care from here on in!"

A head of close-cropped hair bends over him.
What sex? The She/He is Professional.
Al's chair floats free; it's entering a mobile
Of gaping, toothless North American salmon.
His mind, suspended in that silent school,
Slows down to gulp an exit memory. . .

His son pulls out a flask at the foot of his bed

And fills the doctor's cup. They study him
With pity and disgust. His boy speaks up:

"You're right, of course. It's best to pull the plug.
Before, when there was hope, I thought we'd wait
To see if he'd come back."
                              The doctor shrugs.
"But this is damaging to everyone,
especially to him. He's not the type
Who'd take to baby food and enemas."

In deeper sleep Al dreams a pedestal
With his bust crowning it. The monitor
Is there to store and broadcast history,
And all is well with resting now. He slips
Into a playback of his patterned life,
Successes and small faces surfacing,
So many whose luck went bad when he appeared.
the neon word *survive* blinks on, then off.
The moonlight billows, ghosting through his room,
Obscuring the family photos on the dresser.

"Please tell me what to say in my report,"
The Dream-Boss pleads, but God is a tightlipped light,
And Eleanor a mute, absorbing presence.
If only he could speak to her, he thinks,
And almost senses communication start,
Then just as quickly feels the line shut down.
So, her forgiveness won't be as clear to him
As he would like. The room fills up with faces.

No parent-image soothes or batters him.
The League of Spirit Women calmly waits.

"Don't touch the monitor!" a young Al pleads,
as over the Burden Wall the children go,
abandoning their bikes beside the road.

A hand has targeted the monitor.
Exotic feathers spiral up a staircase;
A dead phone line fills up with heartfelt talk
In summer days where listening is long,
And Al relaxes in a plush backseat,
Content somehow without air or radio.
The life he made is shrinking in the mirror.
The anonymous driver downshifts, entering earth-shift.

*

    The funeral is swift. Tom sits alone,
Observes his father's cronies hurry past
For one last glimpse before they seal the box.
At graveside few turn up to bow their heads.
Released from obligation they retreat
To offices where sentiment is slight,
Where Al is one more desk to be removed,
An office to be cleaned and reassigned.
Tom shakes hands with the few who made the drive,
Then walks Elaine uphill, beneath magnolias
In heavy-scented bloom.
                   "Well, he didn't suffer,"

Tom says. "So like him to hurry even death.
It hit him just like I did years ago—
A shock, a burden he wasn't ready for."

Tom grins a little, recalling his father's face.
"It looked good on him. Don't you agree?
With all that make-up on he dropped some years."

Elaine tells how she comforted her aunt
At her mother's funeral. The woman stood
Inside the church door weeping till Elaine
Came close to her and said
                        "My mom looks good,
So good we ought to take her home with us."
Her aunt stopped crying, thinking what a lark
To see her sister propped up by the stove.
So that was one more hurdle they had cleared.
Beside her Tom can taste the smog but laughs.
Elaine locks up her thoughts and drives the car.

      In two weeks, Al's affairs are laid to rest.
Elaine and Tom pack for a sunrise flight
As if afraid they'll be detained somehow.
While pushing on a pair of hiking boots
Elaine sits down.
                  "What kept us here so long?
The child we never had? The work? The cash?"
"My parents," Tom says. "We slipped into their skins,
an obligation, I guess, but now it's done."

*

In Holyhead they check into a room,
Then walk into the sea-town, little changed
In fifteen years. The hills are harder to bear,
Their beauty so intense it wounds the eye,
But the looking cures. The past is far away.

In bed Tom lies awake to watch the moon
And sees the great migrations circling back,
The children home in lands their elders fled,
Back home among their births and burials.
The town clock strikes the hour. It's nearly dawn.
Tom hears the sheep and cattle in the fields,
The blacksmith strike his anvil, the whisk of brooms
On cobbled streets of slowly rising steam.
We're old but we've forgotten nothing, he thinks.
Asleep, Elaine moves close. He breathes her in.
The ferry for Dun Laoghaire sails at seven.

from On Foot, In Flames

Courting Emily

The visitor stands at the grave in knee-high snow.
He's been calling your house since 1962
Asking for you.

Is he a distant or close relation to
That man in Baltimore who annually visits Poe?
Certainly, you would know.

And if this man who calls you should break through,
What loneliness, time, and pain must he endure
At your father's door?

Brushing aside that meddling sister of yours,
He calls upstairs, "Emily, my darling, my dear,
There is nothing to fear!"

Don't greet him in the frills and curls you acquired late,
Long after the Romantics claimed you,
But come down as you

Always were, your hair tucked in a tight bun,
Your limbs loose in drab, light summer dress
The color of afternoon sun,

Sweet Wolf

The armpits and a flare up the back darkened with sweat
(for you have been sweeping all morning), your shoes
Dusty, impossibly small.

Come down to the parlor, dear, and rest.
Don't talk around the corner like a ghost,
Or too sly a host;

That ploy worked well enough on disabled Higginson,
And on ancient Wadsworth, so stiff with God
He couldn't bed you or bend.

Do not descend in a cloud of impossible cadences
And punctuation like slaps to the face—this one is yours,
All man and boy, your poetry toy

Who loves your jokes, and your laughter
Like water lapping in Heaven,
Who would take you as you are.

Still you test his devotion, serving the heavy cake
You made from scratch the night (or half-century?) before;
Your sister returns, the bore.

Sipping bitter tea she claims each word you say,
Or worse, presumes to say them *for* you.
That just won't do!

Your caller whispers in her ear, "Get lost! Your Sis and I
Need time alone, comprendé?" With your taste
For the exotic, the far away you'll never see,

That single, foreign word rings like a wedding bell.
You shoo your flesh and blood away,
If only for a day.

Where and What You Are

I see you in a hundred places. Now
You've gone into the writing where anything
Can happen and nothing is still. If you know
A shortcut to the flesh, a sweet sighing
From the souls of trees that we might make our own
Just say it, so. At least tonight the moon
Is confident. The riverbed is wet
From a summer squall. Tonight I'll make a bet
With you. I'll wager that the hands that tear
The living from the writing disappear,
As will the distance that is like too many
Clothes between us. Braver, unafraid,
You are a light that calms and covers me.
You own me now that you are everywhere.

The Valley of the In-Betweens

Nobody knows the moon as it used to be.
None of us hears a thing:
Not the singing to Christ at evening mass,
Not the joy of sex from the leather room,
Not the scythe of triumph whispering over the field.
Nobody sees the sun, or the light
Crawling meekly under the locked door.
Deaf, blind, too much alone, we
Are late, fearing the feeling of fear
As we tremble in the draft of a high,

Open window, as we sigh at dusk,
As we hide from the mad celebration
Down in the street. At the crook
Of the arm is a bubble of blood
That hesitates rounding the curve of a vein.
In the skull is a cloud,
In the chest is a barn.
Between you and the sticks you must use
To build your house stands a bird of prey,
And a hunter's red eye in the dark.

The Red Ball

Everywhere I go it follows me.
Not long ago I said, at a table of eight,
That I would never feel so much again.
Just then the rough, red sun infected us
Through the picture window.
                              Oh, lighten up!
Our hostess said, more nervous than amused.
Before I made apologies, I said
You won't find me above the crowd again,
Or levitating others, or in the field
Amusing children with my roping skills.

The others who'd had enough were glad to see
Me go. I nodded, bowed and tried to soften
The sound of my clicking bootheels on the floor.
Behind me, rounded faces flushed as if
On fire, while in the yard the hitching post
Had changed into a circle and rolled away.
And so it was I found myself on foot,
In flames, so far away from you I did
Not care that I must walk up one side of
The burning ball, or stumble down the other.

The Pact

> "And I said let grief be a fallen leaf
> at the dawning of the day."
> Patrick Kavanagh, *On Raglan Road*

    Rain bulled into the valley like a giant
Escaping from the pages of a book.
John-Allen in his garden watched it brawling
Over the coastal range. Its highest peaks
Gleamed briefly in the sun that broke above
The Cascade Mountains fifty miles to the east,
Then disappeared in swirling thunderheads.
Behind him his blue house reflected deeper blue
As all the valley darkened, and the wind
Coming in warm gusts that flattened the grass
Advanced on the pear tree, then on himself.
His straw hat blew off, flew crazily away,
Splitting the wicket of two apple trees
Before hanging up suddenly among the roses.
John-Allen still faced west, his hair straight back,
His eyes tearing. He knew he should go in
But tightened his grip on the fence. The storm inside
Would outlast this one, which was beautiful.
A moment's silence, then thunder came calling,
Then all the fury of the storm broke loose.

John-Allen let the rain wet down his face.
He saw the dust on leathery leaves explode,
A grasshopper dive for cover in the grass.
He heard the plastic pinging on raised beds,
And saw her at the back door, under the awning,
Looking out for him or admiring the storm.
He didn't know which, or care, he told himself.
It hurt to look at her, to get up close.
She stepped aside, her eyes still on the storm.
John-Allen stopped, as if to go in alone
Meant he would lose her for good.
Already lost,
He thought. He wanted her to go and stay.
The rain he tramped in stained the worn fir floor.
He hung his slicker up. "Your packing done?"
She sighed, but only the storm would answer him.
He stared into the coil of yellow hair
She always bunched and pinned when she was working;
His head grew light. He grabbed the door for balance.
It's then she looked at him.
"Are you all right?"

"This rain has given me a chill," he lied.

She turned back in, their bodies almost touching,
His shoulder leaning toward her, but obstinate.

"Come in. The fire's stoked, the kettle's on."

His body tingled, polished and alert
From where she touched his arm above the elbow.
He stepped out of his boots and toweled off.
She poured out tea. He trembled as he drank.

"You're shaking," she said, as one might say *you're fine*,
Mixing reassurance with the fact.
He forced another swallow, burning his tongue,
Insisted he'd be all right with a change of clothes.
"I'll get them for you."
                "No, don't bother," he said.

Upstairs he found her suitcase on the bed,
Still open, as if still weighing in the balance.

Her folded flannel nightgown, lying on top,
Distressed John-Allen so his breath got short.
He reached for the inhaler and sat down;
One shot and he was breathing easier.
He touched the nightgown, tracing with his finger
The pattern of embroidery at the neck.
He put his face to it and breathed her in,
Then started at the imagined scent of hay
Turning his reluctant mind to memory,
To the night he pulled in early, noticing
The burned-out light, the darkness on the porch,
The darker stillness of the house, its calm

Unbroken by him calling Sarah's name.
He unpacked papers, put away his clothes,
And sat up hours beside the telephone.
At two he went to bed, the cat at his feet.
Near dawn the crunch of gravel woke him up.
He listened to the key kick into place,
The door creaking on its hinges, then clapping shut.
John-Allen at the window saw the truck,
The driver hesitating, then moving on
While up the stairs behind him she appeared.
He turned to bloodshot eyes above the circles,
The pale skin even lighter than it was
When she was rested. Her eyes told everything.

"You're early." (Sarah began with the obvious.)
He stood his ground, endured the flash of options,
The swift steps closing the distance between them,
His hand, as if another's, flaring up
And sparking in its fury as it crashed
Into her upturned, unresisting face.
He could see her body tense to take the blow,
Her nerves all bunched together to absorb
His rage should it break free and burn through her.
Denying the release of a moment's violence,
John-Allen said no word. Her face grew crimped
And even paler; her straining body sagged.
That gave him satisfaction. He almost smiled,
Then felt like weeping for the sickness in it.

In a moment she came downstairs after him,

Trying to bridge the awful awkwardness
Between them with a flurry of routine,
But as the coffee beans ground down, his question
Vibrated in her as if she were a bell.
"How long?" was all he said, not *who* or *why*.

A knot of raw emotions writhed in her—
Amusement, anger, defiance, even remorse—
Then broke out in a rush of laughing tears.
John-Allen waited for the fit to pass
And stared out at the field where a cloud of birds
Descended, ravenous, pecking the ground
Then swarming up en masse and moving on.
He thought them lucky, all of a single mind,
And knew no humans could ever live like that.
As Sarah calmed herself he studied her,
The way she jabbed at her eyes with a paper towel
And wiped at her reddening nose, stuffed up and swollen.
He pitied her, then steeled himself against it.
They sat down with their coffee, fingered their cups,
Their talk taking shape reluctantly at first
Then shifting back and forth between two poles—
One brimming with aggression, the other restrained.

Inside them there were voices talking, too.
John-Allen's needled him:

What'll you do?
You could kill the lover, your wife, even yourself;
You could stay with her or go on alone.

But how? The thought of starting over ached;
Forgiveness seemed a saintly, distant thing
Beyond his reach.
                        The woman wrestled, too,
With what her private voice was telling her.

Before he knew, just one long day ago,
You found a tension you had dreamed about.
Now you must choose: follow it away
Or stay here if you can. You've loved each other,
You've built this house, you've shared a history.

"We built this place,' she said, as if prompted to speak.
"If you won't talk, if you won't help me now,
I'll have to make out what you mean myself.
Please look at me!" she shook him by the shoulder,
Surprising him with her strength. Like one asleep
John-Allen moved. The subtlest counterpressure
Was enough to render each one motionless,
But still he did not speak.
                                "I can't explain,"
She said, 'why I went out behind your back.
The boy's no older than my younger brother,
Not yet a man. He acted so clumsy at first,
But he kept me company. He helped me out
Those six weeks you were driving Idaho.
Why did we cross the line? I can't be sure.
I guess I felt—I don't mean to sting you
By saying this—as if I were on vacation,
As if we were taking a break from all this...*life*

We've put together. It didn't mean I quit.
I'll tell you, John, the shine came back to us
The more I saw us from far away. It's then
I knew I loved you as I always had.
Now tell me if that means we can't go on."

The sun came up, squeezing the chill from the air.
By noon a yellow haze distorted the light
As seed grass farmers scorched their acreage.
The cows in Frazier's field roamed far to graze,
Then ambled back to the sheds by four o'clock.
A good burn day, they called it in the valley,
A day to stay indoors. John-Allen and Sarah
Had nowhere else to go. They sat talking together,
Reaching the point where nothing new came up,
But neither wished to put an end to talk
For fear that if they stopped they'd never start.

   Not far from there the lover wired himself
On bitter truck stop coffee. All day he trembled
Between his seat and the phone by the register.
His coins exploding on the metal tray
Provoked a glare from the girl behind the counter.
Each time she settled into a hostile boredom
Broken only by curt efficiency
When someone slapped a ticket on the glass.
The sounds of talk and eating buzzed in his mind,
And no call he made got through, not to his boss
To say that he would not be in to work,
Not to his mother, who dozed on beer in her hammock,

Not to Sarah, whose line was busy or off the hook.
He thought of her denying both of them
(A young man's fear of betrayal is like no other's).
He wanted to confess, confide in someone,
But being true he'd kept this to himself.
Had Sarah named him? He shivered at the thought.

Just after five the dinner crowd began
To straggle in—farmers mostly, eating alone,
Or in twos or threes, a few with families.
These last ones hurt the most.
                              Too many people,
The boy decided. Were they watching him,
Some even laughing at his foolishness?
He paid his check and drove his truck due east
To the winding gravel spur of Enos Lane,
Which led him to just a field away from her—
Her property, at least—or was it the man's?
He'd never asked.
                    The valley smoke had settled
By dusk, though some black flakes of ash still floated
Like apple or cherry blossoms on gusts of air.
One landed on his shoulder—a star? An omen?
But he was much too literal for that.
He kept to the line of scrub oak, disturbing sheep
That feasted in the shadow of the blackberry thicket.
He willed his cough away as he drew near
The barn's back door. It opened soundlessly.
He stepped inside involuntarily thrilled,
Imagining that Sarah was waiting there

To stun him with a look of mock surprise
Then move up close, inviting him to touch.
The smell of her hair, the feel of her moist skin
Beneath the summer dress that fell away
So easily, his own clothes slipping off—

But that was all over now. the sick light splashed
Across the sagging floor, and no one came.
The boy stood swaying from the shock of loneliness;
He shut his eyes, attempting to calm down,
Then knelt by the tractor, picking apart an owl pellet.
A starling's indigestible beak and bones
Repulsed and fascinated him. If only
He had made the difficult connection there,
That all life turns on bursts and fits of passion
Leaving behind a clump of broken bones,
A slimy trail, a smear on a patch of earth.
He was wounded, though still too inexperienced
To know all stains are beautiful, sure signs
That life has happened.
      But the boy could only wish
That Sarah would find him there. Yet she'd promised nothing
(How could she? They had so little to talk about.)
And kneeling on that floor of hardened dung
He muttered angrily, then took it back,
His mind refusing to cooperate
With cursing her when all it anchored on
Were images of love. He pitied her,
But much more himself and peered through slats at the house.
He thought of rushing in to rescue her.

Then heard again her voice admonishing:

Whatever happens, you cannot interfere.

Did she know her command had circumscribed his life,
That he'd take her at her word? His future closed.
The hackamore fell softly over the beam
Above his head, the noose efficiently tightened.
The body, calming, swung so rhythmically
An animal watching might easily fall asleep.

*

    Past dusk, John-Allen rolled the huge doors back
And held his breath at the slow revolving motion
Of the body above. He heaved the poor boy down
And checked his pulse, though he knew death when he saw it.
He knew the boy, yet in his shock he missed
The obvious, the rapid steps behind him.
Then Sarah's moaning covered all of them—
The solid, hardened man above the boy,
Herself keening in sickly afterlight.
John-Allen laid the corpse on a bed of hay
And firmly pressured Sarah from the barn.

Later, they talked in the frightened voices of children.
By midnight they had calmed their nerves with drink,
Measuring what to do. Should they call police?
They'd have to leave the valley, and it would ruin
The dead boy's memory; his mother would break,

The locals would be cruel.
                    Toward sun-up he said,
"It's our affair, or I should say it's been yours.
I'm game to keep it here, but you should go.
We'll say you've gone back east to see your people.
Folks will gossip, wondering where you are,
But that'll pass. In time they'll just ignore it."

"But what about now?" Sarah's voice was thin.
He knew she meant the body in the barn.

"We'll lay him down in the addition," he said,
"Back by the window. Then we'll pour s slab.
I'll dig. You read the Scriptures over him."

She stood as if on cue and got the Book.
John-Allen fetched his gloves, his knee-high boots,
And single file they marched to the gloomy barn
Where they made quick work of it. With an owl as witness
John-Allen gently laid the dead boy down.
Removing his cap and gloves, he bowed his head
And listened fiercely to the 23rd Psalm.

*

   The next day's weather broke out cold and clear.
A midnight wind had gusted through the pass,
Pushing the field smoke north to Washington.
On other days like this they'd feel refreshed,
The valley clean, themselves primed for renewal,

But today bore all the weight of what they'd done.
As Sarah scrambled eggs that neither would eat,
John-Allen stared out at the fields and barn,
The coffee getting colder in his mug.
I'll stay with you...her words kept playing him,
But to what march? The blind steps of a fool?
He struggled with his pride, despising Sarah
And hating himself for not forgiving her.
So far, he had survived the thing she'd done,
And would, most likely. She asked for a little time;
That suited him. He said he'd wait a month.
That night he made his bed up in the attic.
Above her Sarah heard John-Allen pacing.
A month would pass so quickly. Where would she go?

In half that time the weather turned to snow
And rain that made the people speak of Noah.
The valley lay unconscious under a cloud
Of cold that penetrated everything.
The creaking out of beds, the straightening up,
The numbing of cold and sleep-entangled minds
Made every morning thick and difficult.
Even so, the valley farmers worked
Their fields in heavy gear. Who prayed for rain
In August now prayed as hard for an end to rain,
For any rip in the horizon's shawl
Of unrelenting gray.
                    John-Allen heard
Some mention of the boy, a question or two
At grange or auction block that tweaked his heart,

But the talk gave way to the waitress's engagement,
The cashier's shame (exposed for tapping the till),
The Lower MacKenzie's polluted salmon run,
And long debates about the spotted owl
Or methods to make burning obsolete.
The boy, some figured, was done in by a drifter,
While others thought he'd simply moved away.
His mother drank more beer, and that was that.

But not for them. Their lives were like a recording
Playing over and over. Their grief was their own.
Sarah forced herself to look ahead,
So each day, with eagerness and manic cheer,
She cooked fine meals and kept a spotless house,
Helped out in the fields if there was need of it
Yet always avoided the barn.
                                            He noticed that
But didn't speak of it. *That's natural,*
He thought, himself finding fewer occasions
To go in there. He kept his distance in all ways,
Working the fields more than he had before
Or parking his tractor to watch the stars at night,
Though nothing he read there made living easier.
Or more to the point, showed him *how* to do it.
Then one day after supper she told him
The time had come. In the morning he could drive her
To the train in Albany. From his bed in the attic
He heard her opening and closing drawers.

*

The day had come. He kept her waiting with work
Outside until the weather drove him in.
Now he lay beside the suitcase on the bed
And touched its spine. His eyes burned in the dark.

So, this is what your pride has made of you,
He told himself, *companion to misery.*
What difference does it make? She cheated you
But otherwise stuck by you. She's tried her best
To make amends, and you've been touched by that
In spite of yourself, and now the further bond
Between the two of you that can't be broken.
What's natural or evil between two people?
You want and need each other. Let it go.

The door half-opened. Sarah hesitated,
Then spoke uncertainly.
                      "John-Allen, it's time."

He couldn't speak. She waited a moment longer,
Perhaps for the suitcase to levitate and float
As in a Disney movie, to her hand.
The silly image faded. She reached for the bag,
And as she closed her fingers on its handle
His own hand, haltingly at first, found hers.
She held her breath, her husband did the same,
And then both hands gripped harder, holding on.
Now nothing was held back, not even words,
As Sarah lay beside him in his arms.

Outside the sky was calm above the farm,
Though to the north the rain had turned to hail.
Over the coastal range a new storm blew.
The fall was ending. Winter had begun.

There Is

In certain Oregon rivers the fish are dead;
Another beautiful stand of trees is cut,
But there is also the morning air,
The new-mown, harrowed field turning
Green, after early rain, in the late fall sun,
And horses nickering for alfalfa when
You first appear at the barn door,
Singing for the lame mare.
There is the tree house under construction,
The barn itself forever under repair.
There is still, for all its shadows,

The familiar light of home, its voices
Comforting from other rooms,
And children on their way to school.
There is always the calendar, not simply
Telling you another living day is through,
But igniting recollections of days when you
Surprised yourself with competency, even grace.
There is blue ink on a cream-colored page,
A blue heron, imperious, commanding
The pond. And there is always you:
What you choose to believe and do.

Levels of Intersection

Rain plows into the Willamette, rushes on.
A young man at a rest stop along I-5
Leans against his Ford Fairlane, smoking.
The sky is robin's egg blue, breaking through
Peaks and funnels of white clouds so immense
That giants might be hiding out in them,
Or throwing parties, or holding election rallies.
Maybe the man travels in a dream of love and money,
Driving to reunion or renewal.
And even if his heart is aching from the company
Of the radio, his journey is not forever,
His uneasiness a momentary weather.
Is that the memory of his mother's kiss
He puts away, the distant look in his father's eye?
Stubbing out his cigarette, does he see
Some welcome waiting for him north of here?

Now take away projection, the things we see
In others that are really just ourselves.
That leaves us with a young man in a Fairlane
Driving away under a clearing Oregon sky.
Who knows what he may be running from or
Driving to? Our intersection fixed the time, one day.
We saw him on his way somewhere, perhaps
To do somebody dirt, perhaps to repair.

Elegy in August
for Beverly

Sleep, little sister, far from pain.
Water smooths stones in the river
As memory calms the chaos
You left behind. Rest easy, sister,
Your babies are older than you ever were.
Even the stain will fade
When none are left to remember
The calls for help you never made.

After burning, blackberry bushes
Struggle up through ash, and love, resilient,
Blooms in all seasons, even for you
Who suffered and could not tell what was right
As you hurled yourself, suddenly
Spiraling upward to darkness or light.

Grateful

Be grateful that you live
Inside the head you do.
How many times have you
Gone sailing through
Your bed or favorite chair to
Wave a sign in the sleaze
Of traffic: *Need money. Please!*

How many times have you
Suffered with the losers
Of war, or chafed and simmered
On a reservation, or brokered
The rescue of many from fear?
How many hours have you
Survived the lessons of gender

Change, or held your hero,
So splendid because of you?
Be grateful, be father and mother,
Be teacher, sister and brother
In all that you dream and do,
Against the day your ledger
Is opened up to you.

My Bird, Your Face
for L F

You'd be surprised. I've trained my bird to be
Your voice. If I could will each face I meet
To be your face, I'd spend more time in public
Instead of in this room, with only the bird
For company. I keep the curtains closed
And go out when the alarm clock tells me to.
I work a graveyard shift. Unable to
Maintain a car, I ride the bus to work.
You see, what time I've left I put behind
Me since that night you cut me open through
The telephone. I'm happy just to sit here,
Unrecognizable to all but the bird,
Ever faithful, greeting me just as you
Used to do: *Hello, darling. Hello, darling.*

For Liam (1949-2007)

When he was young he lived for drama.
He wished himself in a French movie,
Exchanging intellectual, sexist dialogue
With beautiful European women.
One by one, he drove girls far through
The countryside in his two-seater,
The top down even under threatening skies.
"For the romance," he said, "for the drama."

Nobody complained. They drove to get wet,
To shake their hair loose in maddening wind,
To feel the elements on their skin like hands
All over them. *Baby*, they called each other,
And *Toots*. They were doll-faces, sweethearts
Be it rain, be it sweat, it was wetness they
Were after, long days and nights of it,
The romance of it.

*

At forty my friend gave up drink
And got heavy. "It's a shame
That drinking, and the loss
Of drinking, inhibit the drama," he said.
He slapped at his belly, insisting

That touching it was like setting one's hand
Unexpectedly in warm glue. To his credit,
He did this as if he were waving a red flag.

*

Driving home from our AA meeting,
My friend was in a talkative mood.
"I laid down with so many," he said,
"I grew callow and weary
(appreciative, but callow and weary).
I lived the drama, discovering romance,
The dancing on tabletops, the coming
And going and the promise of loving,

"But lately I find that I remember more clearly,
And honor more dearly, the flawed bodies,
The wrinkled, the whittled, the scarred
And varicose-veined, the overweight,
The thinned out, the lovers
Haunted by everything but perfection.
These define romance,
Having many miles of it on them."

*

My friend, approaching fifty, grows quiet,

Though a mutual acquaintance assures me
He is only turning up the volume elsewhere.
I hope so. I could not stand to think
Of his roadster up on blocks,
His fire put out by the torrent of so much drama,
That from now on I must miss him,
My cohort, my spy, my chronicler of romance.

For Lysa, That She May Rise Early
For LM

Each morning between five and six
When twenty serious cows file out,
And the waking cries of sheep
Are the sweetest of the various sounds
That turn night into day,
The world's weather is most inhuman,
Though most secure.
Apprehension disappears—
As if fog to some high ship ascends,
Mysterious as Prague,
As if you could become
One with the field itself,
And the motion of the animals.

After
For AR

Now morning comes. The air at last is warm,
And sleep is gone from your eyes. Turn out the light,
The one you read by, that stayed with you all night,
And step into the world. Silence your alarm.

Turn out the light and look out on the farm
Where wind stirs up the leaves and trees repair.
"Come down to me in your cloud of raven hair,"
You hear yourself repeating like a charm,

But the one you're thinking of is in a dream.
Protect her there, and everywhere, you pray.
The one you love is elsewhere, so far away
Her absence shapes the night into a scream.

Yet morning comes, and though its hours endure
The calendar full of everything but her,
May they also ease your troubles, carry you far,
Safely, maybe even back to her.

Travelers

Because we love the stars
We walk out late to gaze at them.
Because we love the night
We put it on and will not come away.
The stars, the night,
Are all the substance of our thought.
No suffering cries out,
No death comes near,
As time continues on its way,
Remote beneath stars,
Inside the open night.

The Discovery

Under the feeder
Not far away
We found her dead,
The cat, Go Away.

The cat, Go Away,
Our Three Oaks tart,
On a mound of seed,
A beak in her heart.

The beak had a message
Pushed back on its base:
Death to stalkers!
Thus ends the chase.

We nervously scouted
The air all that day,
But the hit-bird got her—
Our cat, Go Away.

This Time of Year

The world practices death.
Our valley fills up with wind and rain
While we who are too poor to have insulation
Have already sealed our windows with plastic sheets.

Blurring the world, we miss our dearly departed.
It's what we deserve, but some
More evenly suggest this life is simply benign
Repetition, a grander scheme than we can know.

The dead lie deep and cold.
Our rehearsals never seem to end,
And our little prayers for summer go up.
A woman of eighty rubs her legs,

A man of forty mimics her.
A child rubbing the sleep from his eyes
Wishes his warmer dreams still held him.
Back to houses the cats come faster

From ditches, gardens, haunted barns,
While sheep, pathetic, scrabble in fields
Baa baa baaing—for what?
To come indoors, perhaps to be cats.

At Home with Doll-Face

We stepped down
Into the little cardboard town.

All day and night
We were posing.

I did not need to water or cut
Our plastic lawn, and I gave up shaving

Because in my Beloved's world
No hair or green thing grew.

My teeth were exquisitely white,
My body fat absolutely zero.

We dressed from designer racks and drove
Our pink convertible to the river each day.

Do you think we yearned for controversy,
Some spice mixed in with the bland stew of our days?

We were deliriously happy, content
With our clothes and gadgets,

Serene looking out at the world's woe
Through the wise eyes of toys.

Paranoid

His daughter's doll escapes
From a box on the table
And follows him to work
In her plastic car.
At day's end she's his shadow,
Frowning at items
He tosses into his basket
At the store.
He can't help watching in
The rearview mirror
As she touches up her lipstick
And jabs at her lashes
With a tiny brush.
Maybe he should wave her
Off the road,
Say to that all-night drive-in,
And buy her a Crush,
And attempt to pry out of her
The mysterious news—
Like what her boyfriend will do
If he sees them together;
Like what his daughter's up to
Out of his sight,
And why a dish like her
Is on his tail,
Always watching him.

Women and Men

Women understand:
Living with it so,
They master disappointment
Better than men,
Who never get the news,
Only its terror.

Living with it so,
Men disappear in cars,
Clubs, and bottles, inside
Their muddled heads,
While women turn on lights
And turn down beds,

And master the disappointment
That men are lost forever
In their fear. If only they
Could be more flexible,
Better in bed, more
Graceful in public.

That's the terror—
That men are almost useless,
That women's hearts may break

On their behalf, then must
Repair to build some peace,
Where men are nowhere.

The Sheep That Feeds You

Lower your face to the platter;
Breathe in the steam, my sweet essence
Mingling with the scent of your own sweat,
As intimate as coworkers crossing an unspoken line,
Or as killer and victim
In the exhilarating rush of opposing intentions.
Lose your senses in the smell of me ripened at last,
Exquisite after the stink of muddy fields. Remember?

All winter and spring you chased me down,
Grabbing among the hysterical flock
For a fist of my wool. You gathered me
To your chest, ignoring the pellets of shit
I let loose in protest (that smeared
the rain-slickered arm pinning a back leg),
And puckered some foreleg skin, hunting a vein
For the injection that fought off three kinds of death,
Or shot a thick solution down my throat
For a new rainbow of worms in my belly.

Did we ever find comfort in each other's eyes,
And did you imagine us coming to any end but this?

I was never troubled so, knowing only the day and night,
The security of the muddy field beneath my hooves,

The gradual, growing distance between my mother and me,
The late-calling, persistent sexual goad.
For my kind there is only the shepherd's truck
And his dog's incredible, hectoring speed,
Steel tubs filled with fresh water, and salt licks
Blessing a patch of dead ground. There is
Only the shade of the one pear tree on a blistering day,
Or the comfort of roof and warm hay in the barn
When it rains or snows, when the night is bitter.

I feel your confusion now that my ear tag's gone.
Which are you? you're thinking.
Is it you, 56? 43?
You know me. Put numbers out of your head.
Breathe deeply now we're together again under Heaven's bright eye.

October

He hung his yellow slicker on a hook
And skimmed the moisture from a windowpane.
A horse looked through his gaze and shook off rain,
Ignoring cows that lumbered through the gate
Like swaying movie stars oblivious
To common measurements of loss and gain.

He wondered where the one true ledger lay—
Inside a cloud, a drawer, an orderly head?
Alone among the commerce of the beasts
He wished that God would coax them into speech.
"Come out and shimmy-shammy with our kind,"
He heard them call through snorts and coughs of steam,

But only in his mind. The moment passed.
Reluctant sleepers sorely left their beds,
Not breaking but diminishing by steps.
Some cursed the cold, others bowed their heads
While from the fields huge banks of fog rolled up;
The dead were stirring, exhaling through the earth.

Daughter
For Jane Mary Katherine (16 January 1997)

This is the day
You come away
With us, meeting
Face to face
The committee greeting
Your arrival. You rush
From acrobatic sleep

On this the day
Your parents say
Thank God! or words
To that effect.
They are skittish as birds
Of the architect
You spring out of.

Jane, you begin this day
To break away
From your cozy zoo
And our busybody,
Good-intentioned say
About all the things
In store for you.

This is the day,
And this the hour
When all is still
But the rain shower,
And the close-up murmur
Of your parents' prayer
As you join us here.

Red Foxes
For Jane

Insomnia pushed Nessa over the falls,
Her boat made of nothing but her own skin.
Deep in the comforter she curled like a baby
Waiting for sleep to return. Under the down
She willed herself a dream, but nothing came.
Nothing but cold and the prickly, pre-dawn stillness.
As fast as a ghost she stepped out of her sleeper,
Pulled on her woolen shirt and knee-high socks,
Her jeans and Red Wing boots. The glowing clock
Read 3 as Nessa hustled to the window
Above the field of young rye grass. The crop
Lay under the fog, straining toward warmer weather,
But winter always stayed too long. she tiptoed
Past her parents' room and down the stairs.
Nessa wondered how they could sleep tonight.

Bundled up in a coat, a hat and gloves,
She headed for the field beyond the barn
And longed for the voice to call her—
                  "Come into the field
Where all of us are living out our time."

Instead, not very high up in the fog
She heard the staggered honks of migrating geese.

They reminded her of students on a bus
Who squirm and *yak yak yak* to steer the time.
And *did* the leader really know the way?
She shivered, thinking *I am not alone.*
Instinctively she angled left and saw
A low shape moving calmly through the mud.
Nessa slowed down, peering into fog,
And met the red eyes glowing in the dark.

"I know you," Nessa said. "Lady Possum,
"Your belly must be empty as a can
To set you prowling so late on this grumpy night."
She matched the possum's pace. "I wish you'd speak,"
She said, "if only to explain your eyes.
Why are they red in the dark? My cat's are yellow.
What color do you see when you look at mine?"

They paralleled each other up the fence line
To the corner where the possum disappeared
In the thicket growing round the apple trees
That Nessa's people abandoned years ago.
She watched the possum burrow out of sight
And thought about the buyers moving in.
Would they have children? *Odds are they'll be improvers,*
She told herself, *removing this nest of vines*
And driving out the birds and animals;
They might break up the farm to sell off lots. . .

Nessa darkened. *They might clear-cut the hill—*
Just like their neighbor down Gap Road, the one

Who never has a word for anyone
Even when spoken to. He puts down traps
For possum, stray cats, skunks, anything
That dares to live where he's put up a fence.
In Nessa's memory, hardly a week
Had passed without the stop-your-heart report
Of his rifle, and many times he'd need two rounds
(the second even worse, meaning he'd failed
to kill his victim with a single shot).

When she was younger Nessa shot a bird.
She was playing Annie Oakley. Her friend Ramon
Had handed her his Christmas BB gun.
She raised the barrel, sighting a mockingbird
On a telephone wire. "One shot," she said.
Impossible. They both laughed at her bragging
As she squeezed the trigger, then the bird fell down.
Ramon picked up the rifle, ran for home,
While Nessa, unbelieving, held the bird,
Refusing to accept the death she'd made.
So that was how easy making death could be.

*

While Nessa walked her father sat in his chair
Between the woodstove and east-facing window.
He felt his years in the hands that held the cup,
In his heart that beat too loudly in his head.

"The bankers must hold papers on the fog

As well as the farm," he told himself. "Damn them."

A sheet of damp wood sizzled in the stove
Then blistered and exploded, arcing through
The open doors to the carpet. William was slow
To move, and in that indecisive moment
Flared a crazy thought. *The house is old,
It's possible.* But sense (or habit) prevailed.
He stamped on the ember, smiling at little burns
That scarred the carpet, a map of almost-fires.
A door creaked open, draft of cold air struck.
"It's Daddy," William said. "I'm by the fire."

Nessa kissed his cheek. He touched her hair
As she laid her head on his chest. She smelled of fog.

"You've been out walking," he said. "Did you circle the field?"

She nodded, leaning back to look at him.

"Come, red fox, be my guardian," Nessa
Whispered, as she had so many times
At bedtime when her father told her stories
Of the woods and fields. "Come, red fox, be our guide."

William turned to the woodstove saying, "Our luck's
Run out. Nothing will lift us up today."

Then Nessa's eyes were wet. She wrapped her arms

Around her father's middle from behind,
Hugging so fiercely it took him by surprise,
His power escaping like water over stone.
Like fog rolling over ditches, she thought.
They stood together, silent, sharing that touch
Until a bell ringing set them both
In motion. William hung the woodstove screen;
Nessa shook out the wheelchair's blanket and pillow
As William climbed the stairs, and moments later
Came down again, holding his wife in his arms.

*

By then the auctioneer was soaking up
A streak of egg yolk with a wedge of rye.
The banker across the table skimmed the paper,
Impatient to go. The older man could read him.

"A minute," he said, "and two more maple bars."

He signaled the waitress, requesting one more coffee
For the road. "I've got to have that kick," he said.
The banker thought of his final college term,
Living on speed as he drove toward his degree.
Now his job was easier. The figures,
The plusses and minuses bracketing his life
Made feeling a cinch; he felt the bottom line.

The auctioneer was different, a local boy
And former football star at Central Linn;

But game days in the fifties were far away.
Twice married, supporting five kids in their teens,
He specialized in liquidating estates,
Making hard times harder, talking faster
To anaesthetize the crowd's collective thought.
Foreclosures were the worst. The night before
He always felt remorse, especially
If he knew the family. But experience
Had calmed him down. The victims on sell-off day
Would suffer their greatest grief, and then go on.
(Wasn't there a famous play like that?
He couldn't recall, his reading days remote.)
It was always the same. The family
Might watch till early afternoon, then leave.

The banker's sudden question made him laugh.
"Has anybody been shot at one of these?"

He picked his teeth. The auctioneer said *no*
And asked if he had ever seen the place.

"Not me. I see it when we sell it off.
Sometimes I wish I worked home loans instead,
But that gets messy, too. You get involved,
You know what I mean? And when the loan blows up
You feel responsible. That's not for me."

*

Nessa's mother smoothed the shawl on her legs

And stared at the fire. She drew a rattling breath
As if to say *I'm finished with this now.*

"Can I get you something, Momma?"

                        "You've been in the field.
You saw them, then?" the older woman asked.

"I stumbled on a possum. I heard some geese,
But dark and fog were over everything.
I felt them in the shadows watching me,
But I didn't see them, no." Nessa wished
That for once she could have told a healing lie—

If only foxes carried us away,
Or wrapped a magic shawl around the farm—

She shook her head, facing the present once more,
And noticed her mother staring, far away.

*

They picked at breakfast, listening to the drone
Of strangers working, setting up the yard.
The auctioneer's assistant shuffled in,
A clipboard in hand, a pencil behind one ear.

"Boss says we'll sell the tools and tractor first."

He spoke, not really to them but just to hear

A familiar sound. It kept him company.
It shielded him from the crippled woman's stare
(he felt for them, but hell, this was his job).
"Most folks are done by two o'clock," he said.
"So, there's our window."
                        Nessa liked that thought—
A window that could suddenly be shut.

*

The turnout was good. Men were there for tools;
Women picked over tables for smaller things—
Kitchen appliances, bedding, handmade clothes,
A chair admired at a social long ago.
Nessa knew the auction etiquette,
Her family's place. Even their neighbors would turn
Away from them, keeping their hands busy.
She knew her job: to make them feel less guilty.
Embarrassing? Of course, she told herself.
She had seen her shame and loss on other faces,
On other days. The things they loved changed hands.
Her mother's face was stony as the quilts
She'd made sold quickly at a modest price.
Antique dealers? Nessa guessed they were.
When a batch of her mother's dresses came on the block
She turned away.
                    Out to the barn she ran.
Standing in the empty, hay-sweet place,
Which looked so big with no machinery,
She traveled back, remembering the summer

Her father and his friend had wrestled beams
Of pressure-treated lumber into place,
Restoring a foundation so delicate
It seemed a gust of wind might flatten it.
And once, while Nessa watched, the jack that held
A section up collapsed, the roof descending
Three feet or so, but holding as the two
Men in the loft yelled out in fear, then laughed
To see the roof intact, themselves alive.

But now her senses told her *look around*.
Stepping soundlessly to the rough-cut door
Of a small side room, she saw in its dusty light
Her father hauling a strongbox out of the ground.
William looked younger than she knew him to be.

It's money, enough to save us,

                                                  she heard him say
Though he did not speak. A rain cloud covered the sun,
And in the purple light the man with his booty
Went into the air like smoke on a damp burn day.

"I'm breathing too much of this barn's old fevered air,"
She said, but there the fox stood at the door.
Then girl and animal traveled into each other
As far as they could, into the spirit's house
Where the red fox said,

                                      "Into the world we're born,
Then out we're called again. Go back to your people.

They need you, Nessa, like foxes need the night."

The fox was gone, but Nessa could hear the voice
As she ran back to the heat of the furious sale.
Her mother was already seated in the Ford
While William stood off by the oak tree with a friend.
She caught his eye, he broke free with a nod.
"I'm ready now," she said.
                              They backed away
From house and barn, quiet in memory,
As the crowd around the auctioneer closed ranks,
Shutting them out, glad to see them going.

*

Southwest, then west by Courtney Creek they drove,
The trailer like a pendulum behind.
They stared, not at the fields around them, but
At years behind them. The sky filled up with clouds.
A soft rain fell as William hit the lights.
They had nowhere to go, only relations
In Washington who could put them up for a spell.
They'd look for a rental, maybe a doublewide
On a farm where one or more of them could work.
William squinted, wiping at windshield mist
With the back of his sleeve.
                         "Stop!" his wife commanded.
She had seen them first, the bareheaded man and his dog
Who were walking without baggage down the road.
Perhaps the man had put his car in the ditch

Sweet Wolf

And needed help, she thought. Somehow, she knew
He wasn't homeless, and even if he were,
What did it matter? They were homeless, too.
They slowed to a crawl, and William spoke to the man.

"It's wet out there. You'd better ride with us."

The stranger nodded, climbed in back with Nessa.
His dog, a tri-color sheltie, sat between them.
Nessa looked them over. Her first impression
Was that the man was young, but now she saw
She couldn't really tell how old he was.
The man looked fit. His eyes and face were good,
So, she stroked his dog, who leaned on her for more.

"He looks a little like a fox," she said.

"That's so," the man agreed. It's then she noticed
His eyes were like the dog's, like eyes she'd seen
So many times in the fields, out in the dark.
"He's always been my guide," he said and smiled.

Nessa's mother turned to look at them.
"It's funny you should put it that way," she said,
"Especially today." Her daughter trembled.

"So, where you headed?" William's nervous eyes
In the mirror were on the stranger.
                              "Nowhere," he said.
"It doesn't really matter where I go;

What counts is how I make out while I get there.
Each day there's something new to lift us up.
Today we needed help, and there you were."

"Yes," the woman in the front seat said.
"That's how it was." She reached for William's hand
And movement out the window caught her eye.
Beyond the stranger's shoulder, in the field
She saw two foxes running easily,
Paralleling the car.
                        Then all were watching,
The dog as well, as Nessa smoothed his hair.
The foxes ran and ran until they vanished
In the longer grasses bordering the field.
At the Interstate the travelers were calm,
Even grateful as they found their way.

Prayer for the Harvest

Tomorrow may we all be light,
Blessed with second sight
That brings the world to us
As children understand it.
The sweet mare in her stall
Will be still enough for all
Of us who whisper our confessions.
Come evening may we sleep all night
In the crooked arm of Mother Time
Where the owl's vigil calms us,
Where the fox in the harrowed field thrills us.
Tomorrow may we all be right
In everything we say and do,
Forgiving ourselves our dispositions,
And those who can't forgive us.

Prayers That Open Heaven

Of a declaration of faith proclaimed among many,
The congregation rising up in song;
Of a lonesome walk around a muddy pasture,
A lullaby boating children to sleep;
Of the bond between your dog and you,
Of forgiveness for those who burn fields
And break promises, who use their power
To lord it over others; of the ditch you dig
With a neighbor, the piles of leaves you rake,
The barn's sure bridge to the past;
Of Our Father and Hail Mary,
Of the sight of a solitary rider
In late afternoon sun on the Cascade Range,
The horse moving like the motion of God;
Of a sky so full of stars you know you are not alone.
What are the prayers that open Heaven, where
Are the words and guides you should follow?
No one answers, no one lifts up your heart but you.

from The World Next to This One

From the Green Pen

One holiday when I was alone, I
Walked through dawn to the edge of town.

It was so quiet and still,
Not even the usual dogs were out.

At my turning point
I stopped under a wisteria arch,

Umbrella of green, purple
And humming of bees.

Then she appeared to me,
A green figure shimmering

Coming down to me
Out of leaf dust and supple branches,

And she put in my hand
A beautiful green seedpod

Shaped like a stylus. It fit
My fingers as if it were made for them.

Long, tapered, firm
Yet soft as velvet, its ink

Revealed all the stories of the natural world,
And I, trafficked in spirit, understood

That they were mine for the telling,
Or not. So, I begin.

All I Took with the Sun

1929. Takeo's Voyage

Because I would not come into the farm,
I left my jewel, Japan, my perfect wife-to-be, and dreams
Diminished as our ship flew out of sight
Down tunnels leading to America.
I thought I'll make my fortune, then return.
I told my troubles to the stars above
And wrote in a ledger, a present from my teacher.
I played cards with a little group of men,
Some of whom believed they'd never see
The shores of home again. Disputing that,
I said that any one of us could be
A man of means, if not of property.

The sea nights conjured never-ending dreams
As I paced wordlessly among the shades,
A Shadow-Boy with no brave song. I mourned
My future, my green past. The shadows spoke
In riddles, softly, whether to conceal
Their meaning, or to vex me, I couldn't tell.
It's bad to be so much inside one's head.

I see now, many years from there, how like
A dish of rain I was, so small and pure

And ignorant, a moony wanderer.
How like the fish the seabirds gobbled up!
So, Fate had marked my brother for the land,
And me for this adventure. That's what it was.
No lofty seeking, but sheer adventuring.
Is that a word? I'm seven decades in
America, and still I panic when
My grammar is uncertain. I met so many
Yanks who made me feel inferior.

*

Seattle, 1929

A beefy, red-cheeked man the size of two
Of us came down to the dock to pick out workers,
But most of what he said eluded us.
It was disgraceful the way he jabbed at us,
But we were tired, grateful to be getting
Off the boat, and so we followed him
To town, to a sprawling boarding house and bowls
Of tacky rice, our first meal in the States.
That night some of us slept on pallets hinged
To rough-hewn walls, while others slept on floors.

Sleeping so, it's easy to rise early.
Another big American was there
To show us work, and by the noon sit-down

We Japanese were Yankee railroad men!
We worked long shifts and volunteered for more
Because the work made tolerable our fear,
The fear that comes of being far from home,
The fear that comes when you're invited to
A party and you show up looking like
The foreigner you are. We worked like that,
Finding in misery a common cause.

*

Hiroko's Passage, 1936

My mother died,
My father, too,
Before I spoke
Or walked the room
Or fought my way
To where I'd be
Across the sea.

On board, my bed
Was by the cook's,
A four-foot plank
That folded out
And dangled from chains.
I'd hug the wall,
Afraid I'd fall.

I knew that I

Had traveled far
From orphanage
To dock, to star,
From empty space
And setting sun
To this new one.

*

Takeo's Vision, 1936

I met her ship. She fell out in a state
Of mourning for the home she'd left behind.
On land again she wobbled for a day.
We spoke in nervous bursts. I couldn't look
At her, while she walked staring at the ground,
Her possessions in a sack I transferred from
Her back to mine; a courtesy, a way
Of showing her that I was glad she'd come,
That life in our new country would be fine.

That night as she slept deeply in her bed
I'd set up by the fire, I felt the presence
Of generations past, as if her dream
Had called them to join us in that tiny room.
By firelight I wandered over her,
But only with my eyes. I marveled at
Her hands and feet, so delicate and small,
Her oval face the color of cherry wood.

I must have slept, for when I woke,

All stiff and cold, Hiroko poured a bowl
Of tea and served it with an almost-smile.
We murmured to each other in morning voices
Thick and halting, the rain a fragrant wash
Outside the open window. We huddled close.
She brushed a cobweb from her hair, and with
That sweeping motion of her hand, so like
A swallow making elegant the air
Inside a barn, my heart filled up with her.

My focus and intentions were so clear
I couldn't wait to leave the railroad life
And lease the farm. I had one all picked out,
A thirty-acre parcel owned by a man
My foreman sent me to. Within a week
My dear and I were married and moved in.

Hiroko's Vision, 1937

The passage hard, I'd had my storm-tossed dreams
About the kind of man collecting me.
He met me at the ship, a falcon-man—
Tight in his body, full of courtesy.
We bowed, and as we walked I studied him
Without him knowing it. His skin shone bronze
In pools of light we entered, left behind.
A time or two I caught a shadow-smile,
And in his features I could see his aunt,
Who with his grandfather arranged this plan.
I saw his posture, straight and fine, a wing

In sunlight knifing above the earth. I saw
That we'd work well together. Our family
Would be the beds we'd make up anywhere.
Watching my partner sleeping by the fire,
I saw that his bones, his flesh, his soul were good.
I allowed it into my heart—our silent pact.

*

The Years

The whistles shouting *work, release, step down*
Were all I knew until my bride-to-be
Arrived. Hiroko cleaned and took in laundry
Seven days a week, but we found time
For picnics at the lake, and Sunday romps
Among the islands of Puget Sound. It's said
The world we toil in of necessity
Is narrow, but the one that opens up
To us through love unfolds like fields of lilies
Rolling on as far as the eye can see.

Soon we became the farmers we were born
To be. Five miles from Santa Rita we
Got down to work on thirty acres of
The richest bottomland I'd seen since home.
We'd beat the sun to work and trailed it back,
And as our crop of corn and beans came in,
We almost forgot: We could not own the land,
Being alien. Oh, there was plenty
Reminding us that we were foreign, strange,

A threat to security, the economy.
We'd feel it in an awkward turning away
While offering to ease a neighbor's task,
Or in a glance we were not meant to see
On trips to town, or on eviction days.
Three times in seven years, our landowners
Informed us they were sorry, we had to go.

So, by lamplight, in late hours, I studied hard
To be a citizen, and in the spring
Of 1941 I took the oath
That made me, with my labor, *American*,
Able to own land. And soon we did.
Down south, near Watsonville, I coveted
A fifty-acre farm. The ground was right
For garlic, artichoke, and Brussels sprouts.
That magic earth, it seemed, could almost grow
A crop without our help. Hiroko said
Our land was giving birth to better days,
And she was right—for almost one sweet year.

Then, early in 1943, a man
Came out to see us from the government.
He did not look us in the eye, but read
From documents he pulled out of his hat.
I didn't follow all he had to say
Because my ears were playing tricks on me.
Like cypress branches, they filled with Pacific fog.

Driving out, his tires kicked up a rock

That nicked my cheek. I wiped the blood away,
And watched his lights grow small. Late that night
Hiroko said, "I'm done with crying now."
She said to me, "You are a citizen."

How did I miss the State's decision? How
Did I resist resisting it? Not one
Of us could fight, for doing so would be
Like a confession, treason in time of war.
The relocation planners might have prayed
For us to rise against them with rakes and shovels.
How easy then to massacre us all.
I wanted to understand. I wanted *them*
To understand, and then apologize.

On a balmy day an army truck arrived
To take us to the train. Hiroko held
Our baby. We carried cloth sacks on our backs,
And on a whim I ran into the house
To grab the sewing machine, thinking we
Could make new clothes as long as we were gone.

*

Hiroko and the Camps, 1944

We did not think, as soldiers drove us off,
That we would never see our farm again.
We rode so long my body became numb
From heat and dust, the shaking of the truck.

Not much was said until we reached the train,
When panic ripped our voices saying *Where?*
Where are we going? Terror seized us then.
The box cars were thick with heat and sweat.
Some women said *Take Heart* and tried to sing,
But soon their voices cracked, their songs sighed out
In misery. In Pinedale we got out
To barbed wire, dust, and barking uniforms
That pressed us into registration lines.
We paced the hardpan yard and settled in barracks,
Some bitter, others optimistic that
We'd soon be going home. For many, the day-
to-day deranged us, even as we set
Up schools and services, elected some
To settle disputes and govern our routines.
We focused on our gardens, sewing, games,
But everyone was drawn to walk the fence
Where dogs would snarl and lunge if you got close.
In winter we were never warm enough;
In summer it was always sweltering.

One positive—we made community
With strangers we would not have known outside.
We women cooked and sewed and cleaned the place
That through our labor imitated home.
Some men would stand around, not knowing what
To put their bodies to. The dust was awful.
It swarmed us, swirling through the barracks boards.
We never got the grime out of our clothes.
One day became another. Nothing new.

Hiss of boiling water, clumps of rice
In earthen bowls, the drinking water warm.
Sunlight thudded against the barracks walls,
Where men, deflated, slouched and shielded their eyes.

Our son turned two on our next moving day.
The bus driver, over his shoulder, said
That he was taking us to Tule Lake.
A few broke down. The rest of us maintained
Our dignity, or so we told ourselves.
Some said we'd like it better by a lake,
And maybe we would be allowed to swim.
That cheered us up until we reached the camp,
Which looked just like the one we'd left behind.
The air like death, the stubble lakebed cracked.

We moved to our third camp in '45,
A higher place, Heart Mountain, Wyoming,
Where Gene was born. The thin air disagreed
With all of us. Both boys were suffering
Most of the time, and many elders died
In the six months we wasted there. At last,
The day of our emancipation came.
We were too stunned, too weak to celebrate
As we made fast our packing, stood in line
For checking out, and wondered where we'd go.
Our homes were gone, so there was nothing to
Return to or revive. Our keepers signed
And stamped our exit papers, and sent us back
Into the world without apology.

*
   Takeo, 1976

Hiroko was our rock and waterfall
In the concentration camps. She focused us
On little things—the daily tending of
A garden plot, methodical raking of
Our compound dirt, the relocation groups
In which we shared the songs and poetry
We could recall. So, we were ready for
The future when it came, like any day.
The trouble was, the future wasn't sure
What it would do with us. A man we knew,
Abducted from Alhambra, said it would
Be smart to settle up in Oregon.
We took his word for it, I signed a lease
To work a hundred acres east of Salem.
In seven years, I bought the property,
Expanded, built a house, acquired two trucks.

So it took me more than thirty years before
My family could buy the farm I'll soon
Be buried on. My darling wife has gone
Ahead, and I've the urge to follow her,
To take my place beside her in the plot
Beyond the barn. My sons have married well,
Two small-boned girls from home who love, like us,
The work and seasons of the land. They have
Strong sons, who have it in them to grow the farm
Beyond my grandest dreams. I am content.

Now that I'm old, my redneck neighbors come
To ask advice about rotation crops,
How they might grow still sweeter onions,
Which markets they should pay attention to.
Enjoying their respect, I tell what I know,
But I keep to myself the knowledge that I am
The hawk that circles their fields, the mystery bird
They admire and fear. I am the dinner guest
They never really know. My family
Is made of this, though I believe it's true
That each new generation distances
Itself a little more from its received
Intolerance, and one day our own blood
Will blossom in a marriage with a race
That scorned and hounded us. The wind chill drops.
After I walk the fields, it's time I slept.

A Woman and Man Stand Alone in the Street

The street is empty.
No human or animal appears.
Even the birds are absent.

They say to each other what
Are we doing here? Where
Is everybody? Lawn sprinklers erupt.

Automatic, the woman says,
Like most of our thoughts—actions
Without meaning, actions while asleep.

And consequences, the man murmurs.
Oh yes, she agrees, always results.
So, what will we do now? The man asks.

Walk, I guess, the woman says.
They slow down at the edge of town,
Listening to a ruckus over the hill.

What do you think? Machinery?
No, she says, it's people, a lot
Of people. Hear it now?

Sounds like marching. Sounds like weeping,
Yelling, singing. Let's go, she says. Why?
Because we're needed. Because we have to.

So That's It

We are all reflections of original catastrophe.
So, the poor in spirit are dumbstruck
As a rabbit of inconceivable size
Is pulled by an even bigger hand
From a hat of limitless darkness.
So, the unemployed go on and on,
Survivors of eons of random collisions;
So, the loveless, wandering in their grief,
Imagine the sweet madness of tendrils
Shooting heavenward in an ecstasy of photosynthesis.
Who lives and who dies?
The cosmos breathes and stars are born, stars go out.
It takes forever as it happens in a heartbeat.
The miracle, I guess, is that the vast soul and puny soul
Are somehow like the centered rider on the trail
Amid solar wind, rubble, and debris,
Their course through chaos the only way home.

Bum God

When God ran out of money he came to me.

"I'm shit out of luck," He said.

That makes two of us, but now I guess
I'm out of God, too.
                       "Imagine," He went on,
"I who made the heavens, the rising
and receding waters and the passing gasses;
I who made life out of nothing, and you
out of burbling slime..."
                            Watch it, I said,
that's mom and dad you're talking about.

"...I who cleansed the world with war—
those were good times! I laughed and laughed.
I made the sun a smart-mouth;
the moon was ice in My scotch. Those I favored,
where are they now that *I* need a little help?"

You can't blame them, I said. You know how it is.
You show up at a party with a cheap bottle of wine
or a 4-pack of *Snapple* and suddenly you're not so popular.

It isn't every day that God drops by to bend your ear

with His whining, His annoying sense of privilege.

"You know I could kill you if I want," He said.

I reminded Him that I, too, was busted. My money
transfigured into liquid and flowed right on out of here—
as He should before I did something we'd both regret.

"Nobody talks to God like that and gets away with it!"

Great big God tears rolled down his hoary cheeks.
It was sickening. Stop it! I said. Be a god!

Hold Your Breath
For KB & PM

Past the breakers Kevin and I kept swimming
After another numbing day of painting houses,
Of climbing up into spidery eaves on ladders
Slick with sweat and oil. It was November.
We'd been warned to stay out of the water,
But we said screw the warnings and screw winter!
We made like water birds in a deep dive
As two ducks floated by in weak light.
Expecting to touch bottom we found none
And surfaced to see the waves flattening out
On the faraway shore. The current had roped us.

Patty, my cousin and wife of six weeks,
Ran up and down the deserted beach
Waving her arms like a bird unable to fly.
Then she sat down to read *Grimms Tales*
Because there was no one around for miles
And what else could she do? We treaded water,
Spotted a dorsal fin about twenty yards off
And decided to swim for all we were worth.
We did that until our lungs ached, then pulled up
To discover the shore no closer.

What a stupid way to die, I thought.
I felt hypothermia overcoming me.
If you think you can make it, go,
I told Kevin, but he wouldn't, the darling fool.
I made up my mind to die and sank three times
Yet clawed back to the air in spite of myself.
When I came up the third time I gasped *Do something!*
Treading water beside me, Kevin yelled *Help!*
In a voice that shook barnacles off rocks.
It was the loudest shout I've ever heard.

Then out of a rise of foam
A boy on a Styrofoam raft appeared.
He couldn't have been more than ten or eleven,
Yet there he was paddling out to us. We grabbed on
And the three of us kicked and scrabbled shoreward
Until we crashed face-first into wet sand.

Crawling out of the tide we lay for who knows how long?
Kevin was up first, panting, shaking, ashen.
When I could sit up, Patty was there, too, crying.
Did you thank the kid? I asked Kevin. No, he said.
By the time I got up he was gone. Patty looked at us strangely.
What kid? she asked. The boy! The boy on the raft!
I didn't see anyone else, she said, just you and Kevin
Suddenly washing up on the beach.

Ever since, when I'm down or thinking of bad endings,
I hear Kevin yelling and see that boy. And I hold on.

Lying Close Is a Crawling in

Baby in her sleep sits up a moment,
Then droops her head to father's neck
Or mother's breast, and kicks methodically
With both feet, up, down, up, down, as if
She'd propel herself back to that place
Of muffled sound and warmth and lazy swimming.

Father leans into his pillow or his wife, dreaming
Of that pure moment when he climbed a ladder
To the barn's highest point just to be able to say
He'd been up there once and knew exactly how it looked
And what went into its design. Climbing in the footsteps
Of the builder who came before him, he imagined

That man walking out of their house every day
To do the work he does himself and thought how
Working well is a folding back, a crawling in.
He dreams of what went into the barn's rebirth:
Hurricane clips, insurance against a big wind,
The Saws-all cutting through wood or metal;

Rotting posts burned beside the graveyard for pets,
Crews of neighbors to raise the walls,
Siding ripped from battens, and cast-iron runners,
Dated 1904, holding up the sliding doors;

Saw horses left out in rain, #8 nails in a left-hand pocket,
The shiny penny he gave one day for a co-worker's thoughts.

Mother wakes early from all the dream commotion
And wanders outside in the gray before first light.
Horse moves in her stall, nickering for carrots
As the woman brings the world into focus, admiring
The field, the big cat hunting by the south gate, the heron
Swooping down to meet what stirs in the breeze-baffled grass.

Talking with the Dead

Remembering Frederick Morgan

Morning. Ocean rain and fog.
I wake uneasy in the Gold Beach motel,
Scratching in my brain to set the day right
And here it is, the calendar reminding me
That on this day a year ago you died.

On this day a year ago you packed
Your gentle manner and disarming clarity,
Your kindness and bawdy humor,
Your high-pitched laugh and pixie face
And crossed over, leaving the phone dead,

The crowded dining room hollow,
The reservoir iced over, the lovers ashen,
The tennis courts deserted.
Ever since I've wanted to get even
With Death. I've wanted to bring you back

Where you belong—a purely selfish act
If I could pull it off. I've wanted to join you,
Loving your company, happy where you were.
Your exit knocked me off my stride,
A rhythm I can't seem to find again.

The Left Behind can't help but make it all about them.
We wade in shadows for answers we can't have,
And though we never left a word unsaid,
I'd give a world to sit with you and talk
Just as we used to do. Now it's in my head,

The work of keeping you alive. Just as you
Constantly renewed yourself (and have again,
for all we know), I keep your lesson close:
Be open, honest, true; be rigorous and loyal,
But most of all be joyful in everything I say and do.

The world is shining even as we lose
The people, things and scenes we cherish most.
Walking on the beach, my son whose middle name
Is yours collects stones and makes up stories for each one.
A life can be a model. I learned that much from you.

Reminder

Remembering George Hitchcock

I remember running into his house on Ocean View,
Full of myself as usual, chattering on and on
About all of the important things I'd done that day.

George sat in a red wingback chair and listened,
Never interrupting, like a man serenely waiting out a storm.
When I ran out of things to brag about he said,

"Today I planted a single row of beans."
I felt so warm and foolish as he smiled.
I felt calm, centered, good!

Meeting Jesus

What's wrong when charming songs for children turn my stomach,
when the voices of those I love feel like coarse sand paper in my ears?
I worry that the motives of friends are impure, that they'll sell me
to aliens if it suits them. My partner loves me, but not enough.

My attorney for the contract dispute just goes through the motions.
My fitness coach makes fun of me behind my back, And God? Well,
There's not much direct contact between us, that's certain.
Years ago, I stood in the kitchen in the big house, the one we lost

when the economy tanked, taking our family business with it.
I was making melon balls for a baby shower. Pavarotti sang,
sunlight gilded the room, and my not-yet-ex-wife frosted a cake.
The mound of melon balls grew until, late in the day, I had hundreds.

That night, dreaming, I saw Jesus for the only time in my life.
I recognized him walking towards me on the street. *Oh my God,*
I muttered, *it's Him! Will He speak to me? What will He say?*
The moment His eyes accepted my confused and adoring gaze,

I knew that I was about to receive the most profound words
I'd ever hear. I leaned forward, and Jesus spoke.
Good luck with those melon balls, He said.
That's it? But He was already beyond me, touching others.

No time for chit chat. No time for *can you be more specific?*
The next day the house filled with strangers and acquaintances.
I hung in the kitchen, drinking too much and monitoring melon balls.
By the time the party ended, the bowl was half empty or half full.

I wasn't sure which, or if it was bad or good. I drank on alone, deep
into the night, avoiding dreams dawning with such promise
yet ending up, somehow, so wrong; but those melon balls *were* beauties,
round and good! So comforting in the mouth, so cool on the tongue.

Autistic Boy
For Temple Grandin

1953.
He isolates himself
In the institution
Where nobody knows
What to do with him.
So, on February 14th
He sits alone,
A pile of heart-shaped,
Store-bought Valentines
On the table before him,
The word "I"
In the upper left corner.
On the empty line
In the lower right corner,
He's been encouraged
To write the names
Of those he loves
And wishes well,
But he ignores the direction
And empty
Line.
In the center,
At each heart's core,
He writes

Over and over
A single word:
Me.

Horse Sense

It's not easy getting under my skin.
Like the others, I ask for little,
A bucket of oats, sweet water,
Maybe a fly mask for a month or two,
And work that feels like work
And connects me to you. A blanket
When it snows is comforting,
As is a song when you brush me
After a long trail ride. I'm partial
To the Clancy Brothers & Tommy Makem,
But Gene, Tex, Roy & Dale will do.
The point is, we warm up space together,
Something rockets to the moon will never do.
You have the earth and all its spells
As long as I am with you.

You
For Sheila Burns

As still as a pagoda, as bright as rain,
You come and go in blue, in black and white.
The sun slides down to keep you company,
Enthralled by your slim waist, your posture
At the bookstore, your feet so delicate
Who would not dream of holding them?
Who would not think of light and radio
When catching sight of you walking through
The town, or desire you when your mouth moves,
Your voice all smoke and shadow?
Like boys romping in the branches of trees,
I swing on every word you say to me.
Your eyes unleash, your smile sweetens me.
Just seeing you unnerves and eases me.

Chess

We sit down for a game of chess.
I am bold with the Queen Mother
As you sip your Johnnie Walker.
What do you think of father
Since the out-patient rammed
Him with that Hummer? Will he be ambulatory?

What was it like, the accident? Gory!
His pacemaker punctured his chest,
And the air bag rammed
Him like a sucker punch. Where's mother's
Passport, by the way? She says she's done with father
And heading off to Paris to become a streetwalker.

Think of that! Mom a tart while dad will be lucky to use a walker.
That's an ironic, ample story.
Shh! Did you hear something? Is that father?
No! Pay attention. We're playing chess.
Sometimes I wish we had a different mother.
You mean, go to a Mother Store and pick one off the ramp?

Yeah, like that! Maybe one with a cuter rump,
Who smiles more and is a better talker.
We sigh. I guess you get the mother
You deserve, I say. At least she's ambulatory.

Remember when we broke into her chest
And found those naked pictures of her with father?

Do you think she's getting fatter?
Why? Because at Safeway you had to wheel her up the ramp?
Is there something you want to get off your chest?
Ha ha! So I spilled my Johnnie Walker.
I am bucolic and self-congratulatory!
Uh oh, someone's coming. I think it's mother.

Er, we're keeping an ear out. How are you, Mother?
We haven't heard a peep from father.
Have you read my ambulance story?
Sheez! She's really looking like a tramp,
Like Halloween candy for stalkers,
Like a porn queen popping out of a pirate's chest.

My ambulatory pecs give me a dancing chest,
While on the ramp I tackle a streetwalker
Who threatens to smother father.

Nicely Done
For MJ

Mark asked me long distance if I'd seen the movie *Sideways*. I said no. It's something special about myself I hold on to, the habit of avoiding the latest rage, but my friend saying see it made me want to. I listen to him, this friend I haven't seen in four years. "It's so much like us," he said. "Just watch it. You'll see."

So one night, surfing channels, I found it on HBO. He was right. I felt stupid about my self-righteous avoidance, and creepy and excited about the uncanny parallels between us, Mark's Myles and my Jack. I bought a previously viewed copy and watched it again before discovering that I could turn on the actors' commentary. Paul Giamatti and Thomas Haden Church are like witty one-liner machines, their thoughts quicksilver, transfiguring into phrases that crack them up and, well, sound pretty hilarious to me, too. It's exactly the same when Mark and I get together! No matter the context, subjects, or disapproving supporting actors, we hurt ourselves with laughter. I feel creepy and excited about the parallels between us and Mark's Giamatti and my Church, and a little confused. Are we like the characters in the movie, or the actors playing them? How many parallels are there? Who are we?

An hour into the movie I step outside my room for a smoke (yeah, I'm One Of Them; I should quit before it kills me, before I kill others with my evil secondhand smoke, and I want to, I really do, but to lie

about it now, well, wouldn't that be too much like the movie?),
but leave the door open so I won't miss anything. Keeping an ear on the actors, I move around to check out the constellations, the moon. It's a clear night so they're all up there, but they're competing with my shadow on the wall. The shadow eerily confirms that my hair looks a lot like Thomas Haden Church's movie hair. "Nicely done," Giamatti says to a Church witticism I don't catch. I'll have to run it back because I don't want to miss an opportunity to chase down loneliness with a laugh. "Nicely done." It's something Giamatti likes to say, an odd, endearing conversational tic, like one who replaces punctuation marks in sentences with *you know*. "I bought a fake Rolex you know..." Like that.

It would be a joy to be part of making a movie you know? You visit new you know beautiful places you know meet interesting people and eat weird food. Best of all you know you get to be someone you're not. You can take as your own someone else's hair you know their mannerisms and style you know even their wit.

Because I don't want to miss anything, I don't stray too far from the door while looking for things in the sky. Fascinated with my shadow and the smoke coming out of my face, I shift my weight from one foot to the other while trying to see the moon through the big tree that hides it. I'm about to give up and go inside when I discover, quite by accident, a tunnel through the foliage crown. It's a perfect sight line, and the moon is in it like a baby at the top of the birth canal, or like true love beckoning from the head of the stairs. I stop shifting and line myself up with it. I open my mouth and imagine swallowing the moon. Instead, a bug flies in, reminding me that appetite often makes us do stupid things. I don't chew. I spit the bug out (not to worry, bug lovers; it survived) and follow my breath up the tunnel. I open my heart to the moon, feeling its power, and it's then that I notice its scary moon face. I want to run inside and lock the door, but the urge passes as the features rearrange themselves. That's better! That's a face I can be with, a compassionate, benevolent face.

I tune back in to the movie patter just as the actors are cutting up about Jack's buttocks—"like two pillows full of milk," Church says. I laugh with them you know thinking didn't I say that once? Did Mark?

The moon is moving. It saddens me, and for no reason at all I'm thinking of a man in Beirut, one of the 25,000 Americans living there who must be agonizing over when would be the right time to take his family and flee. The moon must look different to him, its face full of foreboding. The weight the man carries as he walks inside to stare at his sleeping daughter must be huge. I wish they could all be here with me, sharing some friendship and a few laughs, and maybe on some astral plane they are. Is that the best we can do? Meanwhile you know the moon is on the move. All over the world it's packing its secrets, its warnings and promises, which pour down on Beirut International Airport's smoldering runways and anxious expatriates of many nationalities. It pours down on Mark fast asleep in the south, on me pretending, pleasured by banter like a man in a tree delighting in a beautiful neighbor undressing. It backlights a king somewhere arranging his blind subjects in a circle around an elephant.

"Step forward. Touch the elephant," he tells them. "Now, what's an elephant like?" Their answers are so certain. "Nicely done," the king says. Each one is so wrong you know and so right.

Baby on Fire
For Dylan

I quit the night I set our baby on fire.
I don't remember where we were,
Somewhere in the country, I guess.
Little Gordy, ten months old,
Slept in his car seat behind me
As we drove unsteadily home
After a night of party-drinking.
We were singing, I think,
And I was driving as Winnie sat
Beside me, matching my noise
With alien bellowing all her own.
We were insanely happy.
The windows were part-way down,
I was smoking and singing, and incredibly
Still capable of smelling. Winnie could still smell
A little, too. Smell that burning? I do!
Looking over our shoulders,
We saw our sweet child sleeping
Serenely on inside a baby campfire.
Winnie screamed and hit my arm.
I yanked the car to the side of the road.
We jumped out, opened the back door,
And began beating at the flames with our hands.
Gordy awoke as the last flame died,

Made a funny gurgling sound and passed out.
We were amazed to discover that he
Didn't seem to be burned or harmed at all.
He's like baby Kal-el, Winnie said.
You know, from Krypton.
For some reason, this set us off,
And we laughed by the side of the road
Till our eyes teared up and our sides ached.

Let's Say

What's always left unsaid.

On the parent playing field we stunk it up.
We tried every diet and fitness regimen
that came down the pipeline, but gravity won.
If we'd had the money, we'd have gone for
liposuction, tummy tucks, implants and facelifts.
When we weakened, we compromised.
There wasn't a friend we wouldn't betray
if the personal pay-off were high enough.
We hated our regional managers
and the irritating people we hung out with
in the office and after hours in bars
because we had no place else to go.
We romanced others because we were bored
and they happened to show up.
When people we knew got sick or went broke
we said all the things we were supposed to say
while thinking, *thank God it's happening to him
and not me, that poor, pathetic sonofabitch!*
We showed up at their funerals acting sad and sorry
while secretly exulting: <u>They're</u> *dead, not us!*
Not yet. Not us.

Raccoon and Possum

Raccoon and Possum crept into a house,
Ate the children and went to sleep in their beds.

In the morning they dressed in the dead kids' clothes
And took their places on the school bus.

At recess Raccoon said, tonight we'll eat mother.
On the way home, Possum said, tomorrow we'll eat father.

Maybe we'll drive the car. We'll watch TV
Until our eyes fall out, till we're sick of it.

We'll move out of the house, Raccoon
Said, and live under it if we want to.

When we get hungry, what then? Possum asked.
They stared into each other's eyes.

Circle

Worms connect front to end to front,
Making me writhe and wriggle. I

Swallow spotlights and I'm a star of circles.
Chasing my tail, I run in circles.

I climb a high hill where I make fire
From dry brush and send smoke circles

To neighbors gathered on the green celebrating
The fiftieth anniversary of the hula hoop.

The sheriff's badge is really a circle
With little star-chunks clipped off.

Taking a break, I devour a burger,
That perfect circle of comfort foods,

And think what would baseball, tennis, golf,
Basketball, or handball be without the circle?

The executioner's circle jerks you into oblivion.
Handcuffs are corrective, kinky circles.

The alien in me makes crop circles.
A four-leaf clover is a deformed circle.

Collars, sleeves and cuffs are circles,
As is your logic when you're most annoying.

It really shakes a person up
When you yell *Shut your circle!* at them.

Sand Tray

The point is play. I come, and you go away.
How did it change from last night to this day?

A thatched cottage, a barn of a house,
A jungle man and virgin woman

Larger than my self; the point is play.
I come, and you go away.

Here's Bucephalus, Alexander's world-conquering horse,
A red fox Familiar, stoic and alert,

And a soldier kneeling under a cobwebbed tree,
Cranking his telephone and calling—who?

A black horse, a mare and foal
Flank the saint of animals

While Buddha extends the all-knowing Hand of
Nothingness, Ganesh riding like a sailor on its palm.

The point is play.
Awareness comes, then goes away.

Totem wolves watch and bay.
Lovers lean, temple to temple, hip to hip,

Oblivious to the spirit horse and hooded figures
Walking the labyrinth towards the praying hands

At its core. The Divine Feminine there—
Is there nothing more?

There's play,
Three poet-scholars sharing books and lines

While the Fool and the lion watch
Over everything that comes and goes away.

When the Talking Goes Away Pantoum

What happens when the talking goes away,
When one among us leaves the other in the dust?
I suppose that's when you fill the night
With inner monologues that take you...where?

When one among us leaves the other in the dust,
The rules go *Kaplooie*! It's every rat for itself.
With inner monologues that take you somewhere,
You scuttle after meaning, lonely and bereft.

The rules go Kaplooie! It's every rat for itself
When someone leaps ahead like that,
You scuttle after, lonely and bereft.
You move to the town of the blind and deaf.

When someone leaps ahead in a pretty hat,
She's always leaving you in the dust
In the town of the blind and deaf.
It happens when the talking goes away.

Paddleboat

is a plastic bathtub with foot pedals and a contraption underneath that pretends to be doing something useful like propelling you forward or backward (depending on how you pedal). The toast-shaped back supports don't fit in their slots, and if you're the big one in the two-seater it leans low. Because of that, you ask yourself for the twentieth time that morning if you're fat, and if so, how much you have to lose to be un-fat. You wonder how long it will take and what you'll have to do as you tense your lower back muscles and in no time at all you're hurting. It gets worse. The pain gallops up your spine to your neck, giving you a fuck-over like no other because when your neck and back are sore you're sore everywhere; even your soul is in pain. They take on water, your soul and the vessel you're trapped in; then your old drowning terror kicks in as you furiously paddle until your legs go numb then fall off and there you are—legless, wet, trapped, about to die as the boat churns in pathetic little circles. You know the dainty life vest won't save you, that all it does is keep you steady, face down in the water as you swallow the quiet lake. With all of that volume inside you, maybe then you'll find peace. Maybe you'll be able to relax, free of panic and performance, deaf to the huzzahs of the gawkers running up and down the shore, pointing at you and laughing.

The Day after Labor Day

I thought a lot about teachers and teaching while I waited for the full-time position I believed I deserved. I painted houses and accepted an adjunct job at Antelope Valley College. I liked the name, moved to the desert to be close by, and spent two nervous weeks preparing my inaugural lecture on American Literature.

Of course, I fell in love with my lecture, revising every word until it sang like a hymn, and on the first day of class I entered the room like a god. I introduced myself, took role, and opened my binder. Oh, this is going to be good, I thought. I started at 9:07, which left me plenty of time, 83 minutes, to be exact. I delivered the lecture with style, thinking it was even better than I'd thought. Looking back, I'm amazed that I didn't pause here and there to give myself a hand. Of course, I was doing it in my head. As I reached my conclusion, I envied the students' excitement. What a semester they were in for! I looked up. They looked like the dead. I glanced at the clock: 9:17. My panic felt unique, exquisite. I thought of running, but caught myself and opened the giant textbook. "Ok," I said, "let's open our books to page...97 (that's where I got stuck turning pages), and read till the end of the period."

That night I called my best friend, who was working his own first teaching job in Indiana. "Welcome to teaching," he said. He said it could be worse, I could be there. To convince me, he shared a student paper. "Jesus, there was a man," it began, "feeding the people with loaves and fishes...World War II, there was a war..." It took years before one of my students turned in something as memorable as that. She was writing a paper on the therapeutic effects of horseback riding. "Fabulous pictures pull at our heart strings," she wrote, "showing glowing children in wheelchairs getting mounted." As her teacher, there were so many ways I could have reacted.

I remember a colleague, fed up with the football player who always slept in class wedged into his too-small desk, his head back, mouth open. One day the teacher whirled around and fired his chalk at him. He'd only intended to startle the boy and deliver the general message: *Pay attention! What we're doing here is important!* But his aim was too good. The missile flew like an expertly cast lure into the sleeping tackle's mouth and down his throat. Choking and screaming ensued, followed by a desperate application of the Heimlich maneuver. The student survived, the teacher received a reprimand and probation. That was, by any measure, a lost class.

I could have done something like that with my student, and enjoyed a vision in which I cast a spell that paralyzed her, then positioned a pony on her back as I shouted encouragement. "Isn't it fabulous? Is this pulling at your heartstrings?" Or I could turn a weary, deaf ear and blind eyes to her carelessness and phone in a passing grade. Instead, I asked her to revise the sentence, suggesting that perhaps the horses and not the children should be mounted, that doing it the other way around might actually hurt the children. *Huh?* She said.

Occasions such as these lead to certain conclusions. If you teach, don't be impulsive, brain-dead, or full of yourself. Though your heart breaks over and over, you must not show it unless you can do so skillfully, with a higher purpose and cogent plan in mind. As much as you want to, you must never act out like Cronos, but must channel the patience of river rocks. Teaching is a higher calling punctuated by innumerable *Huhs?* Yet it ends every June, beginning a cycle of restorative convalescence, which teachers wish could last forever, and does until the day after Labor Day.

Dog and Poet

The ghost of Stafford wakes me up
And says let's write a poem, pup.

I growl a sleepy, grumpy greeting
and leave my basket for our poetry meeting.

No biscuit on the table there,
Just paper, pen, and air.

We breathe and as we let it go
We listen for the magic flow

Of cadence and of rhythm
That heals and patches every schism.

When we're done we romp and bellow,
Shaggy me and my Poet Fellow.

A Wee Tonic

After a morning of internet job search and disappointment,
I settle back in my yard sale chair and browse the pages
of a doctor's book on storytelling and chronic illness.
Everyone's dire tale is worthy, and sharing them conjures
A little acceptance and aids healing. Compassion follows,
Or does it? I wish I could take what I know and actively help,

but how? Alone as I am, as we always are, I'm almost paralyzed
contemplating a sister's suicide, a lover's suffering.
Our global neighbors hate us, and I mourn our lost comrade kisses.
So. When must I sell my car and walk my children to school,
five miles there and back, because the budget-cutting bus line
no longer gets out our way? What about Christmas? The rent?

I could use a pick-me-up, it's true. Driving my kids to school,
I'd love to hear Mr. Keillor, after the birthdays and historical tidbits,
share this poem on *The Writer's Almanac*. I'd raise my voice above
the backseat chatter, saying *Eoghan, Jane, listen up! I wrote this poem!
That's right, I did!* and savor the moment as they run to their classrooms,
shouting and laughing, to tell their poetry-loving teachers all about it.

Young Richard on the Road
(for Richard Wilbur)

Our neighbor fed the wanderer and called
To see if we had any work to give.
I met him at the drainage ditch that cut
Between her place and mine. A rabbit dove

Into the hedge where the Bindle-stiff stood
Talking of trains, the barn needing repair.
All day without a word we labored there
Inside the *ping* of tools, the *sussh* of wood

Until I stopped. He stopped because I did,
And side by side we trekked along the fence
Down to the house, a wash, a meal, then bed.
For a week we smoothed corners and banged out dents,

And when we finished the barn breathed easier.
Then Richard said that it was time to go
And turned in early. My sleep was like my water,
Which stung or came down sudden or too slow,

So, I got out of bed. I warmed the damp
With tea, a slice of buttered bread, and stepped
Out to admire the moonlit barn. The lamp
Still glowed in the back room where Richard slept.

I saw him in his long-johns, wearing specs
And writing in a book. I thought to say
What gives? but checked my curiosity
Before I broke whatever spell it was

That kept him working after a brutal day.
I went back up to bed, and when I woke
He'd already gone, his room as orderly
As if he'd never come. A page from his book

Lay on the table under a bolt of yarn.
I found it first and handed it to you
Who drank your tea and studied it twice through;
A poem it was, his poem of the barn.

I keep it in my ledger of accounts
And have occasion, once or twice a year,
To take it out and read it to the horses,
To you, or someone dropping by. No matter

That the man who wrote it is far from here
Or near, living or dead. He understood
That all we are is work if it is good.
Just like his poem, like our barn out there.

New Poems

Acorn, the Clown

I am always living it down, this thing
That Chucko did so well, that Bongo said
To get himself suspended. I am always asked
About it. Is it urban legend? Did he
Really do it? I smile and squirt who asks
With my loaded lapel daisy, and if my victim
Doesn't hit me or chase me, we have a good talk.
I say sure, I felt sorry for Bongo, but not much;
He should have known better than to assume
That his mike was off. He shouldn't have quaffed that snooty
At the commercial break, but he liked the taste
Of the stuff, and you can't tell a clown a damn thing.
It's a clown's nature to be out-of-bounds.

I never wanted to be one, a clown, I mean.
Then I dated a girl, a graduate of clown school,
And I was intrigued. She made me laugh, coming
To bed wearing her bright red clown nose,
and yes, I also got her pissing flower in the face;
I got it lots of times. When we were good,
We were a laugh-riot, but as the laughter died,
I began to see her tricks for what they were—
Hostility. Passive-aggressive is another term for clown.

But all rough edges go bye-bye with time.

I was in the Midwest, down and almost out,
When someone in a bar gave me a good tip.
"Be a rodeo clown!" she said. "It's seasonal
& 40k a year!"
      She'd done it for three seasons,
And only quit because she broke her collarbone.
"I'm going back," she said, "when I'm out of pain & shipshape."

"When you figure that one out, call me," I said.

"Huh?" she said.
Still, I took her advice.
For me, it was larceny or play the fool,
So, there I was, tricked out in greasepaint
And stupid clothes, running for my life
In those hideous, too-big clown shoes
While trying my best to save some cowboy's ass
Who had just been dumped by a bucking bronc
Or bull. Without trying I broke twelve bones,
Enough, I figured, to quit the rodeo, but not the clown trade.

Ever hated something so much you couldn't give it up?

That was me and the greasepaint, me
And the loud silk pajamas, me & those damn shoes
That made conspicuous *thwuppa-thwuppa* sounds
Everywhere I went.

I realize I was sick,
I know I was wrong, but I got a rush
Scaring the shit out of people, especially kids,
And making them laugh at the same time.
There's nothing more dangerous, I tell Jane,
Than a clown with a chip on his shoulder.

"A clown with a chimp on his shoulder?" she says.

I laugh. I consider it and see she's right. Yes, a clown
Is that scary, able to manifest his inner chimp
And put it on his shoulder and leave it there,
Making others edgy. I made fun of Jane,
Then did what clowns always do—stole a good idea—
And so began working parties with my monkey.
People loved it when he pelted them
With banana chips and pissed down my back.
He was darling on a tricycle, but once
(I swear I don't know what got in to me)
When I called attention to his boner
At a birthday fete for tots, I thought
We'd never get out of there alive.

He also fell in love & grabbed a kitty once;
No happy ending there, so I ditched the monkey,
Dumping him at a rest stop on the Interstate—

Monkey-not-see-monkey-not-remember-you—

I repeated this mile after mile as I drove away,

& by the next town, I felt jungle-free, a solo act again.

I found a cheap apartment, settled down
& papered walls with flyers—*Clown for Hire*.
I played at birthdays; I played for businesses.
Schools loved me, too, until the love went dark
With all the evil luck that's said to hang
Above a clown. We only spoke of it
At clown-gabs, where we said things to
Each other we never told to no-bo-clowns—
Those that never had a big red nose.

What did clowns confess? One cried about
His family, how they disowned him for being
A clown.

One clown's wife couldn't stomach him.
She hated clowns!

Another, however,
Couldn't get enough. She slept with clown
After clown until to her the fraternity of clowns
Became so sinister and sad it stopped,
The meetings, the cook-outs and confidences.
That wife moved on, and all was well again.
Family glue was missing in our make-up kits.

It was rather funny, and really sad how we made kids laugh,
Yet those of us who had kids never saw them.

*

Unhappy people drink to steal away,
Telling themselves a monumental hurt
Is just a scratch. Some people drink to blur
The monster's face that lurks in every mirror.
They drink to turn sobbing into laughter—
Those heartless canyon chortles of the not-quite-sane.
Nobody laughs like that more than a clown
Who drinks with other clowns or drinks alone;
He's masked behind the booze *and* greasepaint.

So, yeah, I'm saying that clowns are separated at birth
From the truth.
Jane, are you awake?

You have to hate yourself to be a clown—
Mimes without grace, grotesque to contemplate.
So, you start out in the clown trade hating
What you do, and you get worse and worse.
You're meaner to your co-workers,
Who notice the precise moment
When your lyric laugh turns harsh & nasty.

*

I always told myself there were lines
I would not cross, not ever, yet here I am
At recess, the children incoherent, urgent,
The day muggy, watching from the forest's edge.

I'm here because last night I felt the hatred in the crowd
And I was afraid. So many want to be the mob that kills
The clown that takes their children, and why not?

You know how it started. Somebody dressed up
Like a clown (a clown!) on a dare, or a bet,
Lurched out of woods bordering a school yard,
Waved money at the kids, made noises, threw candy.
I thought all night about that fool
And felt a clown volcano dialing up, and I know
Something you do not: it takes a clown to catch one.
So, I have work to do. If you see me in the woods,
I pray that you shoot clean and true,
Or take the time to ask if I might be a good clown,
A clown that wants to set things straight. To stay ready,
I sleep in my wig and skullcap, my big red nose
That honks when I roll over on my face.

You see my tricks. I love showing off—
Is that what you think? Sorry to disappoint.
A clown is always hiding, is always guilty
Even when he's doing nothing wrong.
So, all I need to do is hide out in
The shadows till my shadow reappears.
Then we'll see who waves the cash around
And leers under a tree.
                        A kickball rolls
To a stop in the wet, rotting leaves at my feet,
& here comes a Johnny now to pick it up.
I see my chance; I seize the kid and go.

No! It's not me in the glowering wood.
I don't know how to hurt a child. My brand
Of fright is all Pretend, a harmless freak show
Where safety and escape are built in everywhere.
Mothers, fathers and friends are everywhere,
And if a clown or two has 'tendencies',
Well, we have an intervention group for that.

The clown the cops are looking for is rogue—
The worst clown of all, worst because
He takes the disadvantage all clowns have—
We are grotesque—and makes it so much worse.
It's why good clowns will never shield a rogue,
Especially a rogue that hurts a child.
Just the story—with no one missing
& no bodies found—is enough to turn a whole town
& every age group against us.

*

When I was a boy, I knew a younger girl
Who almost *was* abducted by a clown.
It happened in the middle of a crowd.
It was high noon. The clown was chattering
And had hold of her hand. "Run!"
The clown said, and they began to run,
But two teens tackled him and set her free.
She said her parents grabbed her up and left
So fast she never knew if it was real
Or all a lousy joke. She never knew

The sex of the clown, not that it mattered,
Though the energy-read made her pretty sure
It was a man. But then what? Did the clown
Go to jail? Did he get away, spinning a plausible yarn?
And if he did, for the moment, get free,
Did he give it up, his fetish, after such a close call?
Or did he stalk her childhood, vowing to get even
& finish what he started?
       One can never be certain
About what a clown is thinking.

If you see one, hold tight to your child's hand.

Career Change
For MJ

I stand outside Nordstrom's, a shadow
And less than half the man I was.
My wrap-around black glasses hide
And call attention to my sightless eyes.
My grey overcoat hangs on me
Like a shameful rebuke;
My porkpie hat ages & shrivels me.
But I have a snazzy cup,
12 Palomino Blackwing pencils
and a special sharpener in my pocket,
Which Mark sent me after
I told him about the operation.
The pencils are super-sharp,
Not to put too fine a point
On it, but be careful when you reach
For one because they'll draw blood.
They'll prick you like I used to do
When I had all my marbles,
Which I lost when the docs drilled
The hole in my skull & out they came—
The marbles, martinis, memories
Good & bad and everything else
Rotting up there in that attic of bone.
If you happen to come by

And I don't reek too much of urine,
Make a little small talk,
Buy a pencil for 5 bucks
And walk away feeling a little better
About yourself, glad that you
Aided a throwback, pathetic
Sonofabitch reduced to selling pencils
With what's left of his half-wit noggin.
If you're from out of town
And live in a wee village, maybe
You can take me home with you
And get me a job of work
As an idiot who comes
With a snazzy cup & 12
Ultra-sharp, Palomino Blackwing pencils.

Bukowski—When I Met Him

When I met Bukowski, I beat him
3 straight times arm wrestling.
I let him win the 4th time
I felt so sorry for him
In his stained, smelly tee shirt.
He stunk like a dirty old man
Even though he was only 41,
But then, he was born that way.
He knew it. We all did.

We forgave him because he said things
We wanted to say to our parents,
Teachers, bosses and anyone else
Who pushed us around.
"When the sun gets in my face
I slap the shit out of it," Bukowski said.
"When the moon puts on lipstick
& wiggles around in tight jeans,
I fuck her till her dark side lights up."

He said all kinds of crazy shit,
But the closest we got to saying such
Things was reading them in his books
Or nodding approval at his readings.
Yes, we all wanted to be like him, but none

Pulled it off. Still, I could take that asshole
At arm wrestling, and that's something.
"Go ahead and crow," he said.
"Sonofabitch! You earned it."

Pissed at Bukowski

I woke up at 2 a.m. pissed at Bukowski.
I rolled over half expecting to find him there
Snorting with his deviated septum,
Farting louder than the floor fan,

And if I had I would have killed him.
But the bed was empty except for me,
And I remembered that the poor old guy
Was already dead. I thought of his smell,

Then, not now, and almost made myself
Sick with it—that old man stink. Of course,
Bukowski smelled like an old man in his crib.
He got a head start in the stink game.

Don't cringe when you read this.
Bukowski wouldn't. He loved talking about
Smells, the fouler the better.
He didn't believe in limits and gardenias.

He loved his women insulting, stinging,
With beer breath and a three-day stink
All over them. In a dark bar
He always took the back booth,

The smelly one next to the john.

Boxing with Sylvia Beach

Boxing with Pound wasn't as easy
As you'd think. He was wiry.
He was quick and for a poet
He could take a punch.

Smacking Joyce around
Was like punching a croissant.
Sure, you could make excuses;
Yes, he was half-blind but...

Hemingway wanted to knock your head off
The moment he put the gloves on. He'd
Punch out his own mother if she got in the ring.
Come to think of it, he hated his mother.

Other than Hem, McAlmon was the best
Boxer among them, but who cares now?
It's a shame. For some reason,
Nobody pays attention to McAlmon anymore.

Sylvia Beach was tougher
Than all of them put together.
She was selfless and committed—
She just looked at you and you fell.

A Great Adventure

My name is Henry Stanley and I am weary.
This jungle lasts forever. I am persecuted
By the mosquitos of Tanzania. This foul river
Makes the air so soupy-thick
I can't breathe.
                    The river goes on and on,
As does my dour Scottish faith, which drives
Me forward, I suppose, to find that crazy Livingston.
It takes a lunatic to find one, I tell myself
By firelight, alternating between smoking my pipe
And laughing like a loon. The moon climbs up, up
Forever, and I am dumb to tell you why
Nothing makes me quit—not the mass desertions
Of my guides and equipment bearers,
Not the death of my thoroughbred,
Whom I loved better than any person ever.
He died from the bite of a tsetse fly,
Yet in dreams we're robust and happy
Cantering through Piccadilly.
Some dreams go on forever
Through madness and fever,
And when I burn brightest I see how my life
Swoops and veers from one desperate chance to the next.
How else to explain my reluctant service
To the Confederacy, my presence at the Battle of Shilo

Where I was taken prisoner (of course!),
But got out of prison with a promise to fight
For the Union. I escaped even that hitch,
Discharged after 18 days because I was ill,
So ill the brass was sure I'd die.
                                        Looking back,
I see I often convinced others I would soon die.
What peculiar, useless talent was that?
Well, it went on, my stop-start life.
After the Civil War I joined the US Navy,
But it only made me restless, so I began
To write, became a journalist (a bum with pencil)
And organized an expedition to the Ottoman Empire.
I was soon in prison, as anyone might have guessed,
But again, I dodged a lengthy sentence.
I talked a good game. People wanted to help me!
I even managed to get money out of Ottoman officials
For some of my damaged equipment. Resourceful?
Well, yes, one must admit I had that! Or must one?
Perhaps all I ever had was dumb luck. I mean,
I should have died a dozen times before I died.
These are just more fever-thoughts as I lie
Beneath a useless mosquito net. In a moment
Of clarity, I wish I'd never left Zanzibar, yet
Here I am, not well trained and ill-equipped
To tackle the wilds of Central Africa for Livingston.
My nights of illness go on forever, as does my name

For this wretched, gorgeous place. It's
The Dark Continent because I said it was.
Go. Look it up.

Diving in Super Cave for Divine Feminine

Where is karst, the limestone land in me where it's always raining?
Where is the sinkhole big enough to swallow a battleship, my ego?
Find a sinkhole that size and I'm close; find
A sin-hole and dive down, cleanse myself of the almost conscious
Missteps I've taken and still take, taking too much for granted.
Such a professional sleepwalker! I should have badges, certs
For my bungling, for my willful indiscretions. Not that I need to
Beat myself up as I'm falling, freezing, rapturing
In darkness that settles down after the deepest dark we know.
Well, you always wanted to be swallowed, so here you go.
Shall you take a new name? How's Jonah? How's Nada? No.
You'll have to make your own name out of the chasm,
Out of the fathomless depth. Way down there no glow stick
Will get you out, no wish will set you free. You're just you,
An on-your-own Me. Go down quietly. Look around.
Touch every little thing yourself not least of all as if
You're touching your Beloved. Woman up.
Become the man you want to be.

The Great Translator

As promised, Clay brought his Vallejo translations
To the get-together and sat like Buddha
On the living room floor. Sizing us up, looking,
He wondered which neophyte he was going to fuck.
Taking off a shoe and sock, he inched a foot forward,
Inviting us to crawl over the shag carpet & kiss it.
Nobody did, but I think one or two wanted to.
I wanted to chop it off, but my machete
Was in my trunk. I kept it there in case I met
Anything on the road that needed killing.
Clay & his kind most assuredly needed killing,
But I never got around to killing Clay or
Anyone like him. That's how I wounded poetry.

Mise en Abyme

Aren't you tired, puny soul,
Of all the knowing that you think you know?

Whirl away down, a spinning top
& sip at the heart of a buttercup.

Remember singing, lights & applause,
The pleasure that you were part of a cause

In sunlight, rain & rue
That lied or told the truth about you

That nothing hides the gulf between
The creature you were & might have been.

Gang of Chimps

I disappeared for two months
& ran wild with a gang of chimps.
My agility & hirsute appearance
When undressed made my assimilation
Easier than I ever imagined. I thought
I'd have to fight my way in
To the Chimp Inner Circle, but no.
The chimp jury was divided,
& a couple had the hots for me.
I was watched & I was reckless,
& I discovered unexpected pleasure
In walking on my knuckles from time to time.

I pursued the chimp gang life because I lacked a mentor,
And gang life is self-medication for the lack of one.
We patrolled the borders of our "land"
Every day, marching menacingly
In single file, 8 to 10 of us in a squad.
Except for the occasional inter-gang tussle,
I saw little action, except for one night
When a gang of Bonobos crossed our boundary.
I guess some of their females wanted a potluck dinner,
And what a coup to show up with fresh chimp meat.

The day they attacked I should have died,

But my gang brothers saved me. About
The treacherous Bonobos I was ignorant.
I knew nothing about their habit of greeting
A stranger with sex, so when a handsome Bonobo
Showed up beside me in line and made lewd advances
(we were all bisexual), I thought, why not? He had
A winning urgency and confidence about him,
& I was happy to let him lead me into the bush
Where he and his pals, as soon as we were out
Of sight, would have torn me to pieces.

But as we veered out of line, hand-in-hand,
The jungle shook from Chimp Gang warfare.
No matter how much I desired my faux suitor,
True to my colors, I had no problem
Turning on him with murderous intent.
I'd taped a box cutter to my inner thigh
For occasions just like this, and I used it
With more than enough skill to negate
My enemy's superior strength. All I had to do
Was dive to the ground & slash his leg tendons,
Rendering him immobile and easy to kill.

Well, that little business did away with
The last reservations that some of the chimps
Harbored about me. I was in deep
With my chimp gang, and even had my pick

Of a little den of females that regarded me
With new respect and desire after hearing
All about my fighting ability. If human
Women secretly love a murderer,
Chimp girls put it all out there.
They want a warrior and a winner.
'Strike first and strike often'—
That's what Chimps, male and female, always say.

Of course, I've had to be careful
Coming back to humans. Not everything
I learned in my chimp gang is useful
Among these hairless primates
(I'm not always successful remembering
that I'm one of them, especially in dreams).
I travel far in my jungle dreams,
Back to my roaming place in line,
Ready to kill at the drop of a leaf.
I dream of the female whose heart I broke,
The family I might have had, and often
I wake up in a rage, chattering
Like a blood-thirsty ape. It's not attractive,
And it could be dangerous, I know,
But it's who I am now.

The Man Who Took Over

The man who took over our town
Was busy all the time, with so much
To do. Because of the things he did
The flag came down. Children starved.

Some insist that he cut to pieces
The body of a migrant worker
Under the shade of the apple trees;
Others say no, he only poisoned the orchard.

Some say he tied the ecstatic girl
To the schoolyard fence, then struck
The match that swallowed her. Later,
He rolled in the ashes like an animal.

Another is absolutely certain
That he loaded a .410, opened
The cage door, and shot the eyes out of Lucy,
The irritating town bird.

Some ran into the church to hide. Others
Ducked in to get out of the rain. A few
Changed appearances, others their names.
Some said *Eat Me!* Some said *Forgive Me*

While the man in charge ripped billowing
Laundry on his rampage through our backyards,
And drove stakes through the outlines
Of charcoal people on our barren lawns.

War

The sun comes up, an eye detects alarm.
The field erupts with thunder, running horses,
While men drive us, intending to disarm

The pestilence that bears down on the farm.
The breakfast curdles in its steaming courses
As the sun comes up and eyes detect alarm.

Survivors gather round a hilltop cairn.
The children wail, their blocks all in pieces,
While far below men struggle to disarm

The terror. The undead appear. They roam
The country roads. The scent of apples teases.
The day warms up, a bird detects alarm.

At last, the only sound a windblown can,
Then quiet so sudden the air inside it freezes.
Some men showed up but failed to disarm

The thing that flattened them. A worldly harm
Is the only thing the ticking clock discloses.
The sun goes out, no ear detects alarm,
And none arrive intending to disarm.

Dancing Truth

Listening to the inspirational podcast
I followed instructions
& began to dance my truth
Around the living room
I felt it   Truth
Taking shape in uninhibited movement
Despite my being the size of a lumberjack

Spinning I saw Cat's face
Watching me
From the sofa
With a look of pure disgust

What the Hell are you doing

I could hear him in my head

What I shouted
I'm dancing my truth

I went on   some steps   some twirls
But stopped   flushed & ashamed
I looked at Cat
But he looked away
Imperious   haughty

Maybe personal truth
So difficult for others
Needs to be kept inside
Restrained   tied down
A secret

It's not the popular view perhaps
But at least one cat believes it
& would have it so
& who knows but he's the one
Who knows

Meteni
For AL

In Latvia on one special day
Goblins wearing conical straw hats,
Two onions & a carrot
Tied around their groins,
Storm out of the forest
Creating a measured chaos
With their staffs as they
Beat the bushes & trees.

The goblins come out of the forest
To administer mild spankings
To women in layers of heavy woolen coats.
The goblins chase the women through the snow.
The women fall down in the snow
& play their parts—the mildly spanked.

On their feet again, sloughing off
Snow & their natural reserve,
They dance with local men.
They drum, they dance & sing.
Frenzied with fertility,

The goblins push on to the town,
Stopping at cottages along the way,

Which they enter as if they own them
& pay special attention to the girls
& women of the house. These
they also spank, mildly.

So it goes, the Day of Meteni
& a curious rite of spring—
mild spanking in the snow.

If Only
for FP

If only Norman Bates,
With the strength
Of a homicidal maniac,
Broke free of the dead
Janet Leigh's boyfriend
And killed him
And killed her screaming sister,
He could have mummified them
And kept them in the root cellar
As company for his mummy Mommy.

If only Ethan Edwards,
Burbling with race-hate,
Had picked up Natalie Wood
And smashed her
To captive pieces
Against the cave entrance wall,
And packed her mangled body
Back to "civilization",
Then people could have
Departed the theater
Questioning their heritage
And hating themselves,
As they should.

If only Jesus
Had come down
Off the cross
Saying sorry,
I just don't feel
Like hanging around,
Who would we turn to
When we need someone
To justify our bad deeds
And wretchedness?

If only Dorothy
Had struck an alliance
With the Wicked Witch
Instead of with
That do-gooder, Glinda,
She might have been able
To ditch the misfits
She was hanging out with
And become princess
Of the flying monkeys.

Late Maker of Chariots

So, the late maker of chariots harnessed the horses,
And drove them hard on the highway to town
Not caring if others in cars would contest them.

Some gave a wide berth, some stopped and stared,
While others, hoping to spook the horses,
Drove close and heckled and inflamed him.

With a flick of his whip he discouraged them.
With a *quick! quick!* he inspired the animals
As hecklers retreated or fell away awed.

In the wink of a cloud he was by them.
In the rap of a hand he was young again
As he leaned ever more on the chariot guard

Between him and his horses, becoming more himself;
They galloped and snorted, tossing their hair
And shredding the years that had bound them.

So, free as the wind once more, they swooped
Through the traffic of the bright busy town,
Late maker of chariots, homeward bound.

The Bishnoi Trees

They came from everywhere.
No one in the village stayed behind.
A few trickled in from distances,
Walking days to show support
Because they saw their future
In their neighbors' end.

The tree-cutters came, too,
Undeterred by fellow feeling,
Comforted by good pay & bonuses.
Packing in tools, armed with rifles,
They came by the busload
To cut & to kill if they had to.

Some said they would never do it,
But others said they saw
No difference between killing
A tree and shooting a man,
Woman or child who would not
Climb down out of a tree.

When shot, they fell like overripe fruit,
Especially the children, and landed
With organ-squishing thuds.
Under the trees they lay

On the cool, shaded earth
Like grotesque broken dolls.

Soon enough, the shade,
The bodies & trees
Were all gone.
Only some stumps were left
Where men sat in the hot sun
swapping stories.

Father's Mourning Wood

It's not what you think.

Across the road from our tract house
Stood a gloomy forest, a place
My father walked in to get away
From the job he hated and the wife
He couldn't talk to anymore.
'My Mourning Wood', he called it.

I don't know if he was being ironic,
Chuckling inwardly about his
Big timber and the tall trees,
But I know he went there
To get away from all of us.
Did he go there to get away
From himself, or find himself?
I don't know. I wasn't him.
I'm still not.

Sometimes he would take me by the hand
And walk with me into those woods.
I was terrified of the dark,
Afraid of the woods and him,
But I went, dutiful daughter,
Because he needed me

And I needed his grief
To write these poems one day.

Even now, in bed by my husband,
I dream about the Mourning Wood,
Long gone to the developer,
As dark and wounding and healing
As ever it was in my father's time
When he lay down on rotting leaf mulch
And toadstools and stared up at the branches
Mocking and dissembling his life.

Like Our Fathers before Us

Before birth, our children visit us,
Appearing in our dreams
As we would be if only we could change
The past, revising the first slap
To a caress, and teach our elders,
So busy demolishing earth and air without a tear,
The sympathetic knowledge of trees.

What mirror will your child hold up to you?
What image will he see as you explain
How you voted and paid taxes for designs
That stripped and drained the options from his life,
Or worse, retreated through TV until
A world you never dreamed of walled you in?
Impossible, you say, there is still time.

And yet, this morning, shaving, you see a face
Much older than the one you put to bed.
You hear your son cry out in his slice of yard
(restricted zone of pleasure, with Fear on the fence),
"I want a horse, some pigs, and black sheep, too!"
You comfort him with bacon, a Galway sweater,
Then bend to model airplane parts and glue.

The boy sits pensively, just watching you.

Rock Gongs
For Dylan & Eoghan

Imagine being the players who
Five thousand years ago

Banged on the giant boulders
At Wadi Abu Dom

What were you playing
What message were you sending

Out of the mountains echoing
Through the foothills

Reverberating across the valley
Then there was water

In the valley and underground falls
Gushing out of the hills

There were people close knit
And carping keeping tabs around the fires

There was intrigue and unspeakable behavior
There was beauty and restorative grace

Your people lived, loved, and died
And the boulders kept saying and sounding

Until the last of you laid down
Going back to the mountain you came from

Imagine that mountain sleep   the hills
And valley sleeping and always changing

The coming and going the casting
And remolding heroic deeds and dust

The desert covers every story when it's
Old enough the desert the preservationist

The desert remembers every player
Every season of drought and water

Every son and daughter gets the chance
To play in this the oldest of human stories

How to reach someone how to touch
And feel and hear so that it lasts

Even in the seasons of forgetting
Folded into the envelope of dust you become

Becoming is a long delicious story
And you are in it now so strike the rock

Paterson, the Movie

I have to stop going to new movies
Because nothing happens in them anymore.
Take this one, for instance.
It's about a bus driver in Paterson
Whose name is also Paterson.
When he's not driving his bus
He's writing poems that sound
An awful lot like William Carlos Williams,
The famous Modernist Paterson poet
Who was also a doctor. When he's not
Driving his bus or writing poems
In a cool notebook he carries around,
He's waking up beside his beautiful wife
Who is Indian or Persian—I'm not sure which.
How could I know? There's no explanation
For her being the only exotic beauty
Living in that neighborhood. It's like
She just popped out of a bottle.
When he's not waking up beside
This gorgeous creature, our bus driver/poet
Is eating Cheerios at the breakfast table.
He's walking back and forth to work.
He's drinking one beer every night
In the neighborhood bar. Every night
He ties the dog up outside the bar,

Which may explain the only thing
That really happens in this movie
In which nothing happens, but I'll get to that.

Only one thing in the movie excited me—the wife.
She's a knockout! She has a thing for black
And white; she designs their entire world
In patterns of black and white—even down
To the cupcakes she bakes for her husband's lunch.
She orders a black-and-white guitar
Because she dreams of being a country western star.
She looked awesome in her cowboy hat!
I yearned for just one scene in which our sad sack
Of a poet/bus driver made love to her, but how
Could that happen in a movie in which nothing happens?
I'm sure the director agreed with me. Why else
Would he work so hard to make such a static movie?
Is art static? There is one scene where the wife
Paints black and white patterns on her dress
While she's in it, the dress, I mean. But,
Now, the one thing that *does* happen. They go out,
The wife and husband, to a black-and-white movie.
When they come home, they find the husband's book,
The secret book in which he writes all his poems,
Torn and chewed to bits all over the black-and-white floor.
Not a single inspiring line is left, not even a legible word!
The wife, who believes her husband's poetry is great

And should be a gift to the world, truly grieves for his loss.
She punishes the dog, too, making him sleep in the garage
For a couple of nights. The sad sack husband becomes
A super sad sack. It suits him and the movie. For the last
Ten minutes of the movie he mopes around, sitting down at last
To stare at the Paterson Falls and (I'm guessing) his own
Pathetic tumble. He sits there, looking, thinking (I guess)
And a Japanese man approaches. He sits down with his copy
Of Williams, a bilingual edition and asks a few questions
About his favorite poet and Paterson. He also shares
That he, too, is a poet though nobody has ever heard
Of him in America because he has no translator.
He gets up to leave, begins to walk away and turns back.
He gives the bus driver a beautiful book with blank pages.
Ah, so! He says (I'm not making this up) and smiles and leaves.
Our 'hero', sad as ever, opens the book to virgin pages,
Clicks his pen and begins to write. That's pretty much it.

In a minute the credits role and if you last that long
You'll see that Ron Padgett wrote the bus driver's poems.
That's a cool little footnote for a movie in which nothing happens
Except for a variation of that ancient school joke—'the dog ate my homework'.
I can't help feeling that this movie would have been better
With a subtitle. *Paterson: The Dog Eats His Poems.*
I almost hurt myself quiet-laughing as they came home
To all that canine destruction. The dog ate his poems!
Hysterical! Still, I don't think I could recommend
This movie except perhaps to the guy on Death Row
Awaiting execution for raping and killing his own mother.

I remember thinking one more thing...I thought
I hope Padgett made a shitload off this mess.

Shit

Doing the menial shit he'd always done,
Up to his elbows in shit, Dad would say
Shit! Shit! a thousand times a day
While stay-at-home mom drank herself
Into Shit Land watching soap-shit
On their shitty little black-and-white TV.
For twenty years they went at it,

Mom throwing food on the table saying *Eat Shit*,
Dad catching her looking at him funny,
Hissing *Oh, yeah? Shit on you!*
They did it, dad told him, *for* him
("You little shit!"), so that he might marry well,
Get a good education, and a job
That would bring in lots of money.

Cat Killers

I'll take care of it, Lydia said,
And went out to the barn
Lugging a 5-gallon bucket of water.
Rollo watched from the back door
As she struggled, leaning to her left
Like a comma, like an old woman
Balancing on an invisible cane
As the death-bath splashed
Over the bucket's rim.
Rollo wondered if the water knew
What it was going to be made to do;
Was it protesting, trying to escape?
Lydia disappeared into the barn
And Rollo retreated inside
Where he chain-smoked in the kitchen.

Half an hour passed before
Lydia returned without the bucket.
She was pallid, like a heroine
In a Poe poem or like one of
Bela Lugosi's movie lovers.
She stuck her head in the sink
And threw water over it
And gouged and rubbed
As if she were trying to scrub
Away the memory etched in her face.

When she was finished,
Rollo handed her a towel.
She savagely dried herself,
Then gave him a look that said
My accomplice, you swine!

When she spoke, she said
I'll never do that again!
There were tears in her eyes.
They kept mewing, she said.
They tried to climb out of the bucket,
She said, and I kept pushing them under.
It took forever! Rollo hugged her
But she pushed him away
And would not look at him.
By midday, all on their own,
They'd accepted that something between
Them was broken.
Next time, Rollo said, we'll do
Something different. Next time.

Next time, a month later,
They accepted the offer
Of the lady umpire and potter
To come over with her .22
And shoot a new batch
Of feral kittens. I'll pop
The mother, too, she said.
That'll put a stop to it.
She was country,

She was matter-of-fact,
Even cheerful as she
Went outside alone
And opened the prison cage.
Pop-pop-pop! That was it.
Done. Lydia and Rollo
Stood in the sunset kitchen
Shaking, unable to move,
Wanting desperately to get
Their hands around something—anything
They could salvage, anything they could fix.

Growing

He outgrew everyone he knew.
He outgrew his apartment,
The street he lived on, the town,
County, even the state. He
Outgrew his degrees &
Everything he'd ever learned.
His toolset disappeared in
The Grand Canyon of his hand. He
Looked at his family & saw nothing
They were so tiny. He outgrew his clothes
& went naked; he burst out of his truck
& left it stranded on the side of the road.
He outgrew the left bank & the right,
The algorithms & catechisms,
Even the middle of the road.
He outgrew philosophy & psycho-
Therapy, time travel & the speed of light.
He outgrew the redwood
& the spirit walkers
& the spongy tomb of the brain.
Family? Empathy? Friends?
He was too big for that, too big.
He'll be bigger tomorrow than he is
Today. And you, hummer-buzzer,

Dandelion, Worm-face,
What mountain will you wear away
With your frantic wings?

Her Uncles Come at Christmas

I quickly grew tired of the game they taught me,
The one where I stuck my hand deep
In their pants side pockets for loose change,
My hand burrowing like a shrew
Until it met tree root, as they called it,
And I finally wriggled & wrestled free
Of that cave goo, my palm & fingers sticky,
My face wrinkling as I smelled my hand
While they laughed and laughed.

Christmas is the happiest time of the year!
Someone cried.

Almost every year, one of them
Would stay over. Then I could always
Count on an overnight uncle crawling
Into my bed when all were asleep.
They must have attended the same
Niece-fuck school because their M.O.
Was always the same. In the scary,
Uncly dark, the big smelly body
Would scrunch me like taffy
Around a peanut and begin
By purring "The Night Before Christmas"
In my ear. They were breathy;

They were poor reciters, &
They sweated old man smells
That made me ill. But I believed
In the season's spirit, so I gave,
Or gave up, whatever they needed,
Which cost me more than I could know.

Her Shoe, Her Foot

Walking home after school
the boy climbed up
to a second-story balcony
& jumped off just like Guy Williams
or Guy's double playing Zorro

Two older girls clutching school books
watched him and giggled but the boy
paid no attention until one girl
kicked off her shoe and said *pick it up*
Flush with gallantry & courage he did

Put it back on she said
& bending low on one knee the boy
looked up at the pretty older girls
Their faces peculiar   happy & cruel
as they laughed at him kneeling

Kiss it first the girl said *kiss my foot*
The boy bewildered stared at her foot
Disgusted & excited he threw the shoe
At her and ran
The girls screamed & cursed him

All the way home he ran

where he locked himself in his room
& curled up on his bed panting & sweating
He lay in the shadows wondering
Had he escaped something shameful or missed his chance

When The Reaper: Ode to a Lit Mag
for MJ

When *The Reaper* came out scything
Many poets broke down squalling.

It was Autumn. Leaves were falling
In Kentucky where the gunning

Editors, fierce & punning,
Taxed the lady who lay out sunning,

Her supple patience tuning
Out the brouhaha, all that laughing

Of *The Reaper* with bottles tilting.
Oh, the happy-go-lucky swilling!

What they argued & all the writing
To them, and others, too, was thrilling.

On poets & pretenders, dead & living
They kept dishing.

It was fun, the fakes dissolving,
All the troubles they were solving

And the bar that they were setting,
Levitating, ever rising.

Did they ever think of stalling,
Wearing out, two blackbirds cawing?

On the plain, the summer broiling,
Roasted poets screeching, crawling

Grabbing backsides stung from thwapping
While the brawley boys kept swinging

To the sound of joyful singing
As *The Reaper* kept on scything.

The Calapooia Flood

Harmon

When the dam gave way, I'd been up an hour
Drinking coffee, getting the stove to burn.
I didn't see it. I heard it and smelled it.
It rumbled low and mean. Like mold it smelled.
I went to the door and looked up past the barn
And saw our neighbor's house coming slow
But coming on. I hollered to my wife
Who was still in bed in her slip with our baby girls.
I used my trouble-voice to get her up
And I figured it was good because dog gave
A little whine and tucked his tail. Those ears
Of his went flat, and I was on the move.

I jumped into my overalls, no shirt,
No time for it, and really started yelling
At the foot of the stairs. The woman, almost naked,
Came flying down with a child under each arm
And we were out the door and standing in
A swirl of rapid water up to our knees.
It's then we saw it, a wall of water, black
And simmering like stinking hell-stew spilling
From a giant cauldron. My wife, she tucked the girls
Beneath each arm and ran. I took my boy
And ran sideways and dove and grabbed and prayed.

When we came up for air I saw Denise,
The neighbor lady two farms up from us.
She stood on her porch in water up to her pits
Yelling "Harmon! Come get us out of this!"
Her house was moving like a riverboat,
And I just watched like I was in a trance.
I turned around to find my family
And as my head was turned I heard her scream.
I looked that way and saw her raising her arms
And heard her yelling, "catch the baby, Harmon!"
A balled-up blanket flew into the air
And came up plenty short. It made a splash
And bobbed along like wood then disappeared.
I never thought to make a grab for it.
I don't know why. I guess I knew what it was,
But even if I had a doubt I won't
Forget the sound that came out of Denise.
I never heard such hurt in a sound or felt
Such pain as what I saw before she sank
Among the broken pieces of her porch.
I hear that sound and see that face in dreams
Most every night, and always when it storms.
I wonder where the sack came up,
Wonder if the baby and Denise are reunited.
We never saw that dog of ours again.

*

Ardis

I don't know what my Harmon wants from me.
Oh, that's not right. I know exactly what
but I don't care. It kills me to say it. Before
The flood took everything, I loved to cook
For family and friends, and I can say
Without much bragging that my vittles were famous
Around this valley but now...the hunger's gone.
The caring took off, too.
Before the flood
I loved to keep my home all spic-and-span.
I sewed and worked outside just like a man,
And taught the children real good about
Loving God and living by the code,
The one they learned in Sunday School.
I fixed myself up, too, because a man
Deserves to see his wife a beauty
When he works as hard as my man does to make
A place that's safe for us.
I guess maybe
That's why I don't dress up anymore for him
Or anyone. I don't feel safe, and I've a mind
To put the blame on him. Not that he
Did anything wrong. Cripes, I reckon
He did all that he could. But that baby.
Wish he could have hooked that baby
And reeled it in. I admit I look at my own
Kids and feel guilty about them living.
So, some days I stay in bed

Ignoring my kids. I got these sleeping pills.
They're just about my only friends sometimes.
And Harmon? He leaves me be. He's far away
Though I can see and feel him well enough.

*

Denise

Judas Priest! When that dam gave way
It sounded like an airplane landing
In the living room, or an earthquake
Or artillery. I never heard anything like it.
I was making bread, up to my elbows in flour.
My man had already left me a year ago,
And the hired men that I depended on
Were hours away, as was the postman, Jim,
Who stopped in for fun when we were able.
I ran to the cradle in the kitchen door
And picked up the baby, blankets and all,
And wrapped her up real tight like a football.
I ran out on the porch and oh my God!
A mountain made of water was coming on.
It took the house as it was going by,
Just ripped it out of the earth like you'd pull a tooth.
The water was all around us, rising fast.
I knew I was a goner, the baby, too,
And that's when I saw Harmon. He shot up free
And seemed to have a solid enough hold.
I yelled. He looked right at me but didn't move
An inch, not when I begged him to come on,

Not when I threw my baby as far as I could.
He floated on his porch, watching me,
And then my baby in her sack go down.
I wanted so much to kill him, and then myself,
But all my guns in the house were out of reach.
Bastard! I screamed. You miserable son-of-a-bitch!
But then the water met my lips and forced
Its tongue into my mouth, my lungs, my gut.
I fought it hard, convulsing till I felt
My body blasting apart, and then I stopped.
I became the water; the water was one with me.
You realize, crossing over, it's not so bad.
Maybe you regret the unfinished bread,
The botched pass from your chronically weak arm,
And Harmon, who'll suffer more than we will now.
Well, that's his lot. He had a choice to make,
And he picked long-term suffering. He froze.

*

Ida

One moment I was rocking, fast asleep,
Then felt mother's hands all over me.
Too tight, too tight! I squirmed in my restraints,
But what could I, a baby, hope to do?
I heard the most terrific noise outside
And had one thought—mother's crushing me.
I wondered why. Did dough refuse to rise?
Did she look down and find me hideous,
A burden she never wanted dragging her down?

I wanted to see, but I was in a dark
That made it hard to breathe. Then she let go
Of me and I was flying through the air,
A perfect pass to God. I didn't think
That at the time. I knew it when I crossed
From there to here. I flew. I hit the water.
I flew from my mother there to nowhere,
To no creek or lake or river, just forever.
I had no life except transitioning,
The point, I guess, a tragic reference.
So, did I ever make a difference?
Does it matter that I lived so short
A life, without accomplishments, and died?
Was my being born and dying enough?
Long after even the water disappeared,
Somebody from Red Cross put a white cross up.
Some may pass it thinking how lucky they are,
But mostly I think they're thinking they're glad it's me,
Not them. I say that's how it ought to be
We all depart with questions on our lips.
Was mother saving me or killing me?
We met again in water, reattached
When she floated by and bumped me, then grabbed me,
Then died with me. Together, we drank our fill.

Joe

We sat together on benches
Awkward & unloved
Watching heat ripple
Across the cracked blacktop
It was summer   school was out
As you soon would be
Leaving the push mower
Half-fed in the grass
Smashing the front windows
Of the house & running inside
To the sweltering attic
Where you hung yourself with your belt
I was miles away by then
You had gone too
Yet went back to no one
Just the benches
& summer empty & heavy
Nothing left but heat &
The belt around your neck
That held you &
Would not break

Poetry & Literacy

The word cracks in her mouth.
The man is wrong, the State
That made them misleads them.

Sexless voices in microphones
Transfigure media, echoing
And shimmering past conscience,

Past hilltops swarming with followers
Blinded, barely functional
In their smoky clothes.

Barefoot, they are almost bodiless.
Tongueless, they are afterbirths
Of speech, viscera of words.

What sound can they make
But an untranslatable
Buzzing in God's ear?

Anacampserote

Some herbs, supposedly,
Can get this done—
Bring back the ancient,
The heart-stopping one.

A dragon's glowing spine
Streaking the sunset winter sky
May whip up recollection
Or wet the ever-seeking eye.

I've been in love, been loved,
And lost them one by one,
Lovers and Beloveds—
Full moon and chariot sun.

Yet always in a meadow
Of the soul and of the mind,
I take what's green and growing
And cut the ties that bind.

I put them in my pocket
And grind them in my room,
I drink them down or rub them on—
My own horse and my groom.

If ever you return to me
Or I come back to you,
Will we perceive each other
Forever lost or new?

The ANS

A man, I feared that I would fail
Her autonomic neural system's urge to sail.

The intimidation of the pelvic nerve,
Thwarts desire and the need to serve

Her on the mesolimbic pathway
Where she outperforms in every way.

Paralysis of the amateur
Is worse than whips & striking spur.

Disable the vigilance center, fight or flight;
Talk, listen, practice, till it feels just right.

Remember to begin with loving words
And touches soft as the down of birds

All up and down her neck & arms,
Inside her wrists, with a hand that charms

Delicious dopamine from Cupid's arrow
And serotonin by the wheelbarrow;

Sweet oxytocin from her neural barn,
And vasopressin like woven yarn.

But take your time. Don't be racy.
Promise her safety. Show her. Safety.

The Woman in the Painting

She pricks the mind. It sizzles.
Sit down to your plate of brains.
After 20 years, she spoke to him that way
When she spoke to him at all.

*

I don't understand the picture, Millie said,
So many browns and grays and black,
Too much muted blue and yellow. What
Is the woman in the picture doing?
Standing by the road, waiting for a son
Who is never coming home from war?
Has she just buried something in the garden,
Her husband, perhaps?

*

The firm of Marboar and Sniffles said No,
They couldn't imagine the market for a book
About women written by a man.

*

The woman in the painting, a solid, layered

Lump in billowing folds, has her back to me
So that I may never look into her eyes,
So that I may never know what she is thinking.
If I could look into her eyes,
Would I know one thing that she is thinking,
Or would I latch on to a thought all my own
And think it hers? Is that my method
When I'm social, when I'm blending in,
Wandering through the gallery among pictures?

*

Oh, who is that at the door?
I'm not ready to see anyone.
I slept badly. I threw up twice
And drifted in and out
Of a blue, humming screen
That filled my brain with unnatural light.

By the age of 60, dear, you should be over
The need to partner, Mrs. Ballup said.
Really, it's much more satisfying to be alone.
Since Pigeon died I've never been happier.
I don't miss all the cooing back and forth,
The mood swings, then the diaper changes
And the way he forgot my name. Oh,
I admit I envied him his second childhood.

*

I'll ignore the insistent knocking.
When it's gone, I'll shut the curtains
And sit with one sharp light on the painting.
It changes nothing. That woman's going nowhere.
I wonder, with her back to me, if she's thinking that,
Or if she's curious. What am *I* up to?
I wonder if she and I would be friends.
If she did not have the distinction
Of being in the painting,
Would I notice her at all?

*

I have a two-inch cat scratch
On the back of my right hand.
Ancient Dakota gave it to me
Two days ago on my late-night walk
When I too aggressively rubbed his belly
After he rolled over on the road.

*

One day, we will all roll over on the road.

*

I have so many errands. I have bills to pay.
I must go to the bank. I have a hair appointment
And I've scheduled a massage, then at 2,
A pedicure and manicure. It's wise
Having so much to do. Then I know
I am alive, that I fit in this life.
That quiets thinking. The wolves are fed.

*

Hungry wolves stalk the canvas after sunset.
When the woman walks off the canvas,
That will be my signal that it's time to go.
Then I'll be awash in browns and muted yellows,
In blues and black. I won't be fit for company,
But I'll run with the pack and feed when they do.

The man next door is burning manuscripts.
Smoke in the shape of words curls out of his chimney.
The sky fills with words. They soar out of sight, but some
Drift down like pollen, inflaming people unready to receive them.

*

I stand in the road waiting for someone.
What next? What comes? 'Cows
Flow up a hillside, following unexpressed desire.'

No Little Genius

If I'd been a smart boy, perhaps a little genius,
I would have found a way to meet Vanessa Bell
Before she died the day before my eighth birthday.
A boy you read about in Dickens could have
Pulled it off, but not a stupid American kid
Who had no clue that anything existed beyond
The town that chained him,
That called him *mine* and sat him down in school
Each day to break his spirit, teaching him nothing
He'd revere when he was old—like meeting
Vanessa Bell—Virginia's sister—before she died.

Of course, it was always too late to meet Virginia,
Who as she wrote felt the weight of every word in her fingers
And crossed over eleven years before my birth.
But Leonard, her husband, was still around
When I was fifteen! What was I thinking?
Not much. How hard would it have been to fly
To England or hop a tramp steamer to Ireland?
But the Jack London in me was dormant
And would be for years. No genius then. Had I even
Heard of Leo Woolf? I can't say, lacking the memory
Of a genius. That chance also sailed away.

So did the opportunity to cure the cancer

That killed my mother, the addiction that wrecked
My father & the depression that drove my sister to kill herself;
Or the option of euthanizing the lousy men that killed so many
Women everywhere...was it millions or billions?
But I had no genius for any of it, not even a little,
Not a damn drop.
                        Much older now,
I feel the sparks of genius all along my shadow.
They're not spectacular and don't do much more
Than make me work with perseverance & joy
At that which I love most, sharing stories,
Understanding pain and changing bad to good if I'm able.

Virginia Downstream

I would have been there for you
Unlike the fisherman upstream
Who didn't see or do.
I would have seen you.

I would have been there as I was
Sprinting across the parking lot
To pull a boy's hand
From the car door that slammed on it;

As I was reaching into the cab
Of a rolled, smoking pick-up,
Pulling out three kids
And a panicking driver (their father, I think);

As I was when I ran through the snow
to cut off a runaway sled, angling, timing my leap,
Laying out flat and hooking it with two fingers
Inches before it and the three-year-old on it

Zoomed off a steep cliff down into dense trees.
Such were my shining moments, heroic
As I'd always wanted to be. It should be
Enough in a useful life, but I grieve

Incidents that happened without me.
When my sister killed herself
I slept 2,000 miles away.
And I was nowhere to be found

When I could have said to Liam,
'Come on, man, don't mess around;
Put your father's rifle back in the closet'
Or just taken it away from him.

But sometimes I was there
And *would* have been for you,
Somehow overcoming your resistance
& yanking those damn stones out of your pockets.

Virginia's Way

I put my ear to the River Ouse
& listened to church bells tolling under water

In the current there were voices
Of six children playing

In the deepest part the lady's voice
Unvanquished and unyielding   said

(if not to me, to whom)

What took you so long

This way   Come

The body is a mighty feint

The body is a mighty feint
A dodge from there to here
& thought an obsolescence
Transforming as it tears

Through everything you thought you knew
& every unawares
Like waking in a sudden storm
& knowing what is true

About the Author

Sweet Wolf (Introduction by Chad Abushanab) selects poems from six previous volumes & new poems by Robert McDowell. He is the author of six books of poetry, fourteen books of fiction, criticism and creative nonfiction and editor of dozens of collections. His poetry has appeared in journals and papers around the world, including *Poetry, The Hudson Review, Sewanee Review* and *London Magazine,* among many others.

McDowell was also co-founder of *The Reaper* magazine and Story Line Press, the latter of which he served as editor and director for twenty-two years. He is also the founder of the Rural Readers Project and co-founder of the annual international Poets Prize. He taught at UC Santa Cruz, University of Southern Indiana and the low-residency MFA program at Bennington.